Titles by Janvier Chouteu-Chando

The Usurper: and Other Stories
Triple Agent, Double Cross
Disciples of Fortune
The Union Moujik
Splendid Comets
Flash of the Sun
Fortune Calls
Fortune's Master
Fortune's Children
The Norilsk Bears
To Be In Love and To Be Wise
The Fire and Ice Legend
The Sweetest Madness
The Grandmothers
The Hunger Fire
The Shades of Fire
Father and Sons
The Doctors
Dark Shades
Fateful Ties
The Verdict of Hades
His Majesty's Trial
Ngoko's Folly
The Usurper
The Dowry
I am Hated
The Oaf

Non-Fiction Titles by Janvier Chouteu-Chando

FALLEN HEROES: African Leaders Whose Assassinations…
BROKEN ENGAGEMENT: Why a Donald Trump Win…
THEIR LAST STAND: Donald Trump's Upset Victory…
Ukraine: The Tug-of-war between Russia and the West
THE CANARY IN A COAL MINE EFFECT:...
Cameroon: The Haunted Heart of Africa

Cameroon's Unity, Separatism, and the New Cameroon

Janvier Tchouteu

TISI BOOKS

NEW YORK, RALEIGH, LONDON, AMSTERDAM

PUBLISHED BY TISI BOOKS
www.tisibooks.com

EPIGRAPH

"The time for revolutionaries with the complete freedom to maneuver is over."
>   —*CHRISTOPHER NKWAYEP-CHANDO*

Acknowledgement

My deepest, warmest and everlasting thanks to Dr. Samuel F. Tchwenko and Christopher N. Chando for challenging me towards the path of humanity's enhancement.

DEDICATION

Dedicated to the loving memory of Salomon Muna Yakana

Cameroon's Unity, Separatism, and the New Cameroon

Contents

Quotes

"Cameroon is not a country of slaves that no man can free."
Janvier Chouteu-Chando

"Every great cause begins as a movement, becomes a business, and eventually degenerates into a racket."
Eric Hoffer

"We are not involved in this struggle only because we think that we will dismantle this system in the course of our life. We hope Cameroon changes tomorrow. But if it doesn't, we will be happy to know that we made the ground fertile for the next generation that will end the rot in this country, and then establish the "NEW CAMEROON".
Dr. Samuel F. Tchwenko, former UPCist and chief ideologue of the historic SDF of 1990-2002

"The enemy is not the one who is facing you with a sword in hand, that's the opponent. The enemy is the one behind you with a knife at your back."
Thomas Sankara

"However [political parties] may now and then answer popular ends, they are likely in the course of time and things, to become potent engines, by which cunning, ambitious, and unprincipled men will be enabled to subvert the power of the people and to usurp for themselves the reins of government, destroying afterwards the very

engines which have lifted them to unjust dominion."
George Washington

"We know that Africa is neither French, nor British, nor American, nor Russian, that it is African. We know the objects of the West. Yesterday they divided us on the level of a tribe, clan, and village…They want to create antagonistic blocs, satellites…"
Patrice Lumumba

"You see these dictators on their pedestals, surrounded by the bayonets of their soldiers and the truncheons of their police ... yet in their hearts, there is unspoken fear. They are afraid of words and thoughts: words spoken abroad, thoughts stirring at home -- all the more powerful because forbidden -- terrify them. A little mouse of thought appears in the room, and even the mightiest potentates are thrown into panic."
Winston S. Churchill

"...The world gets blessed every now and then with unique souls who though burdened by their invisible crosses, still have the extraordinary strength to forge ahead in life and give others a helping hand at the same time. Despite their tribulations, most of us think they are fine. Even when the weight of their crosses become unbearable, even when they proceed in a breathless manner, we still have a hard time understanding that they are drowning. In fact, we even condemn them for failing to sacrifice more..."
Janvier Chouteu-Chando, Disciples of Fortune

"The greatest difficulty we have faced is the neocolonial way of thinking that exists in this country. We were colonized by a country, France, that left us with certain habits. For us, being successful in life, being happy, meant trying to live as they do in France, like the richest of the French."

Thomas Sankara

"Loyalty to country ALWAYS. Loyalty to government, when it deserves it."

Mark Twain

"A minimum of comfort is necessary for the practice of virtue."

Patrice Lumumba

"They wrote in the old days that it is sweet and fitting to die for one's country. But in modern war, there is nothing sweet nor fitting in your dying. You will die like a dog for no good reason."

Ernest Hemingway

"We find that at present the human race is divided into one wise man, nine knaves, and ninety fools out of every hundred. That is, by an optimistic observer. The nine knaves assemble themselves under the banner of the most knavish among them, and become 'politicians'; the wise man stands out, because he knows himself to be hopelessly outnumbered, and devotes himself to poetry, mathematics, or philosophy; while the ninety fools plod off under the banners of the nine villains, according to fancy, into the labyrinths of chicanery, malice and warfare. It is pleasant to have command, observes Sancho Panza, even over a flock of sheep, and that is why the politicians raise their banners. It is, moreover, the same thing for the sheep whatever the banner. If it is democracy, then the nine knaves will become members of parliament; if fascism, they will become party leaders; if communism, commissars. Nothing will be different, except the name. The fools will be still fools, the knaves still leaders, the results still exploitation. As for the wise man, his lot will be much the same under any ideology. Under democracy he will be encouraged to starve to death in a garret, under fascism he will be put in a concentration camp, under communism he will be liquidated."

T.H. White

INTRODUCTION

The cause for change being pursued today by the majority of Cameroonians (the struggling masses) does not bear its origins from the wind of change (demands for democracy) that Soviet leader Mikhail Sergeivich Gorbachev's Glasnost and Perestroika generated across the world, a wind of change that jolted those political systems that were failing to conform to the demands of world civilization and progress, which place the freedom and liberty of man and the interest of humanity above the twisted interest of the unscrupulous selfish minority.

The cause for change otherwise known as the Cameroonian (Kamerunian) Struggle began in 1910 led by Martin Paul Samba (Mebene Mebongo). Patriotic Cameroonians, who accept one another irrespective of their compatriots' ethnic, racial, religious or regional origins, acknowledge the fact that the first phase of the Kamerunian (Cameroonian) struggle was defeated in 1914 by the German colonial army following the execution of Martin Paul Samba and Rudolf Duala Manga Bell. They also accept the fact that because of that defeat, the land lost a unifying patriotic or civic-nationalist force to ensure Kamerun's unity during and after the First World War (The Great War), a void that played against the Kamerunian people when the victorious British and French colonial powers went about partitioning the defeated German Kamerun after the war.

The lethargy that followed the first defeat of the

Kamerunian struggle and the resultant partition of the pre-1911 German Kamerun into French Cameroun and British Cameroons (British Northern Cameroons and British Southern Cameroons) lasted for thirty years, or the equivalent of a generation, before the divided Kamerunian people revived their national consciousness again. This time around, the revival of the original objectives of the Kamerunian struggle—independence, freedom, justice, development, unity, peace, democracy, liberty, progress, international cooperation and international fraternity—was done with an additional objective of reuniting a land and a people who through no fault of theirs had been separated from one another to suit the interest of Britain, France and other foreign powers.

Reuniting Kamerunians also meant mitigating the consequences of partition and putting the land and its people on the path to realize the original purpose of the Kamerunian struggle embodied in the words "THE KAMERUNIAN DREAM" (CAMEROONIAN DREAM). This second phase of the Kamerunian struggle dominated by the quest for the reunification of British Cameroons and French Cameroun was led by the UPC (*Union des Populations du Cameroun"*, otherwise known as the Union of the Populations of the Cameroons), a legal political party born in French Cameroun on April 11, 1948. The UPC and its affiliated political parties commanded more than 90% of the support of educated Cameroonians in both French Cameroun and British Cameroons and had the open or tacit backing or sympathy of more than 80% of British Cameroonians and French Camerounians before the vindictive and fearful French authorities banned the UPC on July 13, 1955, a move that was backed two years later by the British authorities in British Cameroons when the authorities there also banned the UPC in 1958. With the elimination from the political scene of the party that was the land's most dominant movement and that was the best reflection of the aspirations of the Cameroonian people, advocates for reunification and independence for the lands of the former German Kamerun(British Cameroons &French Cameroun) were in a predicament.

The fact that the UPC was left after its ban with no other option to freely lead the struggling "Kamerunian Masses" to their aspirations, the fact that the colonial powers perceived the UPC as an obstacle in their design and influence over the former German Kamerun, and the fact that its members were being hounded and killed, the UPC finally came to a conclusion that it had no other option but to resort to the path of armed resistance. The painful decision that led to more than ten years of armed resistance contributed enormously in the political evolution of the territories of the former German Kamerun and the partial reunification of these territories (British Southern Cameroons and French Cameroun), but it came about with the death of more than half a million Cameroonians (10% of the population), and it came about with the loss of British Northern Cameroons to Nigeria. Yes, the cause that spurred the fight for Cameroon's reunification and independence resulted in the reunification of British Southern Cameroons and the Republic of Cameroon (former French Cameroon) in 1961, following the plebiscite results in British Southern Cameroons, but the price paid in achieving that was very high indeed—Cameroonians witnessed the first case of crimes against humanity committed by the French Army in French Cameroun and the puppet regime they put in place there after they made French Cameroun a member of the United Nations Organization on January 01, 1960 by granting it independence in a process that effectively made the territory a neocolonial possession of France.

The assassination of the Ruben Um Nyobe (The UPC's leader) on 13 September 1958 by French forces; the poisoning of his successor Felix-Roland Moumié in Geneva in October 1960 by the William Bechtel, an agent of the French secret service; and the execution of the third historic UPC leader Ernest Ouandié in January 15, 1971, after he gave himself up in August 1970; marked the second defeat of the Kamerunian struggle, the successful entrenchment of the French-imposed system under the regime of French puppet Ahmadou Ahidjo (the first Cameroonian president), and a new reality of a pseudo-independence to soothe the pains and emotions of the patriotic struggling Cameroonian masses and to neutralize their civic-nationalism, a very peculiar union-nationalism also called Kamerunism, which is considered an advanced ideal that brings diverse peoples together in a continent plagued by ethnic, religious and racial divisions. The carrot and stick strategy of suppression, intimidation, handouts, extortion, bribery and corruption that the French political leadership under the umbrella of FrancAfrique (France's special relationship with its former African colonies and territories established before it granted them independence) sustained the 24-year rule of Ahmadou Ahidjo, and has been sustaining the usurper regime of Ahidjo's successor Paul Biya ever since he was handed power by Ahmadou Ahidjo in 1982.

That defeat of the second phase of the Cameroonian struggle led to a second political lethargy that even saw the democratic nature of the former British Cameroons undermined after Cameroon's reunification, a process of subjugation that kept the dynamic Cameroonian people docile or politically subdued for two decades.

Today, we are in the third and hopefully or certainly the last phase of the Cameroonian Struggle to realize the Kamerunian Dream of "THE NEW CAMEROON".

That the struggling Cameroonian masses have been whisked off their political lethargy is glaring for all to see; that their determination to realize the objectives of the eight-decade-old Kamerunian(Cameroonian) struggle is clearly and resolutely challenged or resisted by the status quo or the Biya regime and its external backers (The French- politically setup in Africa otherwise known as FrancAfrique) that have been benefitting from the mafia setup called the Cameroonian system, is something the world knows about. But exponents of change in Cameroon know that getting rid of the anachronistic French-imposed system is the only recourse which would allow Cameroonians to build "The New Cameroon" that would involve Cameroonians of all ethnic groups, religions, political affiliations, regions and races in the process of nation-building. Cameroonians know that getting rid of the system is the first step in reconciling Cameroon and Cameroonians.

In power since 1982 is Africa's absentee dictator Paul Biya, who was made the successor of his predecessor Ahmadou Ahidjo by an order from former French President Francoise Mitterrand; Ahidjo, who himself was brought to power by the French to usurp the aspirations of Cameroonians in their liberation struggle led by the UPC that the French banned in 1955, a party with more than 80% of the land's intellectuals and even more national support. France had made sure Ahidjo's power was secured by decimating its support base in a 12-year war against the party and by killing all the UPC leaders (Un Nyobe 1958, Felix Moumie in Geneva 1960, Osendé Ofana 1966, Ernest Ouandie 1971 etc.), leaving Cameroon a nation haunted by an "Unfinished Liberation Struggle". Today, Cameroonians are out to get rid not only of the Dictator Biya's autocracy but also of the French-imposed system that its custodians want to continue with someone else after Paul Biya departs.

Chapter One

The result of the Plebiscites in British Cameroons on Joining Nigeria or the Independent La Republique du Cameroun (Ex-French Cameroun from 1918-1960)

Between 1959 and 1961, a series of referenda were carried out in the territories of British Cameroons (British Northern Cameroons and British Southern Cameroons) to determine not only the political evolution of that part of the former German Kamerun, but to most of all determine the future nature of the sovereignty of these territories. Below are the results.

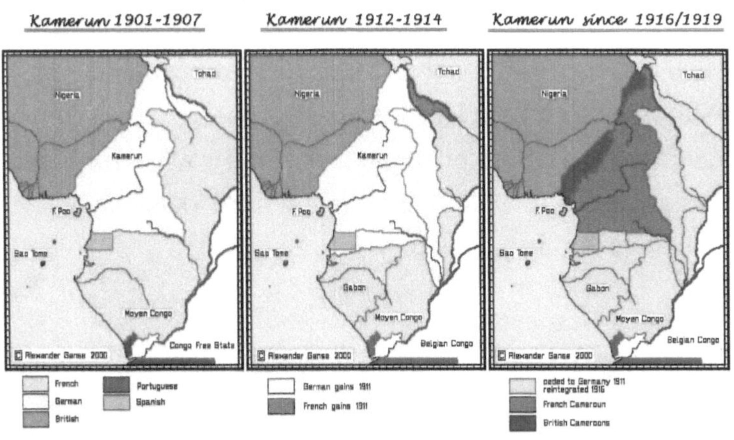

November 1959 British Northern Cameroons Plebiscite

Main Points: Voters were asked if they wanted to join Nigeria when it becomes independent or decide the political status at a later date.

Northern Cameroons

Registered Voters	129,549
Total Votes (Voter Turnout)	113,859 (87.9%)
Invalid/Blank Votes	525
Total Valid Votes	113,334

Results	Number of Votes	% of Votes
Union with Nigeria	42,788	27.75%
Postpone Decision	70,546	62.25%

The February 11-12, 1961 British Cameroons Plebiscite

Main Points: Voters were asked if they wanted to unite with the newly-independent Nigeria or the newly-independent La Republique du Cameroun (Ex-French Cameroun from 1918-1960) when independence is granted to the two regions.

Northern Cameroons

Registered Voters	292,985
Total Votes (Voter Turnout)	Not Available (N/A)
Invalid/Blank Votes	Not Available
Total Valid Votes	243,955

Southern Cameroons

Registered Voters	349,652
Total Votes (Voter Turnout)	Not Available (N/A)
Invalid/Blank Votes	Not Available
Total Valid Votes	331,312

Results	Northern Cameroons		Southern Cameroons	
	Number of Votes	% of Votes	Number of Votes	% of Votes
Union with the Federation of Nigeria	146,296	59.97%	97,741	29.50%
Union with the Republic of Cameroon	97,659	40.03%	233,571	70.50%

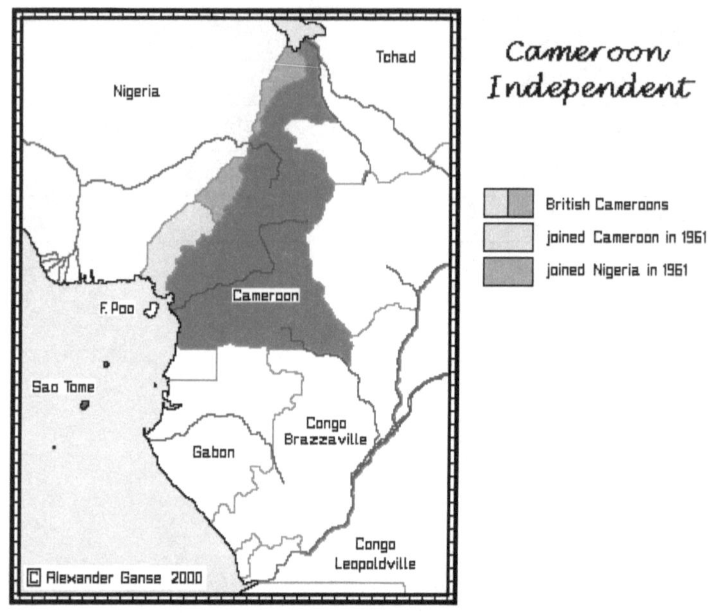

The result of 1961 Plebiscite in Southern Cameroons (From EA Aka, 2002, p.278)

Plebiscite district	Nigeria	Cameroun	Total	% for Cameroun
Victoria				
· Southwest	2552	3756	6308	59.5
· Southeast	1329	4870	6199	78.6
· Northwest	4744	4205	8949	47
· Northeast	3291	9251	12542	73.8
Kumba				
· Northeast	9466	11991	21457	55.9
· Northwest	14738	555	15293	3.6
· Southeast	6105	12827	18932	67.8
· Southwest	2424	2227	4651	47.9

Mamfe				
· West	2039	8505	10544	80.7
· North	5432	6412	11844	54.1
· South	685	8175	8860	92.2
· East	1894	10177	12071	84.3
Total (SW)	54699	82951	137650	60.3
Bamenda North	8073	18835	26908	70.0
· East	1822	17858	19680	90.7
· Central west	1230	18027	19257	93.6
· Central east	529	18193	18722	97.2
· West	467	16142	16609	97.2
· South	220	19426	19646	98.9
Wum				
· North	1485	7322	8807	83.1
· Central	3644	3211	6855	46.8
· East	1518	13155	14673	89.7
· West	2137	3449	5586	61.7
Nkambe				
· North	5962	1917	7879	24.3
· East	3845	5896	9741	60.5
· Central	5059	4288	9347	45.9
· South	7051	2921	9972	29.3
Total (NW)	43042	150640	193682	77.8
Total (Southern Cameroons	97741	233591	331332	70.5

Chapter Two

Cameroon's Unity and the Dreams, Fears, and Hopes of the Kamerunists (Union-Nationalists)

The union-nationalists of Cameroon are pragmatic revolutionists, progressive reformers or radical evolutionists. These are men and women who grew up being what they are more as a confection of circumstance than of what was bestowed upon them by birth that gave them a social identity. These people greatly developed or did not suppress their human touch. Unlike most, they do not find it easy to live without the slightest spasm over the pains and suffering of their fellow compatriots. Unlike most, they have put their purposes far above personal considerations and even above their personal interest, an uncommon quality. By dwelling on their sense of humanity, they consider the alleviation of the pains, turmoil, and nightmares of their compatriots over the alleviation of their personal well-being. It is because of their all-embracing humanitarianism and deep awareness of the Cameroonian reality that they accepted the fact that the demanding task of alleviation cannot be based on individuals who are so many and complex as separate entities. Cameroon's union-nationalists are acutely aware of the fact that the task of alleviation should be for the entire Cameroonian people. They know that Cameroonians have been dishonored, oppressed and traumatized en-mass and not separately.

Permit me to call Cameroon's union-nationalists the advanced Cameroonians. These exceptional groups of patriots, who have been shaped by circumstance and have a clear sense of the meaning of life, have never been allowed to the helm of power in the country's political life. With legendary origins and a gruesome past, they are the best reflection of Cameroon itself. Cameroon's union-nationalists are aware of tribal, ethnic, religious, cultural and linguistic sentiments; however, they have not allowed these to blind and overwhelm their reasoning for a progressive Cameroon. They are aware of the fact that Cameroon's chronic malady lies in its anachronistic institutions, complete dominance by France and a detached oligarchic leadership. It is the different sentiments and workings of the French-imposed system that has shaped individual Cameroonians to varying degrees and constrains them in their drive towards authentic change and progress. However, Cameroon's union-nationalists in their advanced ideals are those exceptional compatriots who have detached themselves from the shortcomings of the system and the blinding sentiments of tribal, ethnic, religious, cultural, linguistic and social ties. They stand as the epitome of the renewed Cameroonian.

Since becoming a distinctive entity under the German colonial rule eleven decades ago, Cameroon has occasionally conceived of liberation movements that would have advanced the nation into a better position had these civic-nationalist forces been successful in their cause.

In 1910, Martin Paul Samba (Mebenga Mebono), the first Kamerunian civic-nationalist leader realized that the progress and glory of the land rested more in a future that was devoid of colonial control and permeated by progressive Cameroonian concepts. He began one of the earliest liberation movements in Africa and the first in black Africa. However, time and fate cut him short in his campaign to rally the full support of the peoples of Kamerun. Cornered by the German colonial army near Ebolowa in 1914, he opted for surrender rather than face the massacre of his people. On August 8, 1914, Martin Paul Samba was executed, a day after the execution of his close friend and ally in the name of Rudolf Duala Manga Bell. That was the first trauma to Cameroonian civic-nationalism in the hands of the German colonial army, leading to defeat in the first phase of the Kamerunian struggle and to dormancy for its nationalism for years to come. It was such a deep trauma that even after British and French forces defeated the German army in Kamerun in 1916, no civic-nationalist force emerged to defend the territory from partition by the victorious European powers.

This partition into British Cameroons and French Cameroun and the ensuing mandatory rule unfolded consequences of a disruption of past economic, political and cultural ties, as well as their resultant usage. Moreover, it is the shortcomings of partition and the disruptions that are haunting Cameroon's unity today. The imposition of separate English and French administrations in the land as agreed in the mandate formula only created systems that had little in common with pre-colonial experiences and that were out of touch with Cameroonian reality at the time.

Yes, it was due to the regrettable partition that Cameroon's civic-nationalism was rekindled three decades after, with a union content this time around in its quest to reunite British Cameroons and French Cameroun. It began in French Cameroun in 1948 under the UPC (Union of the populations of Cameroon) and spread over into British Cameroun where OK ((One Kamerun) and the KNDP (Kamerun National Democratic Party) championed it. The goals of both the English and French-speaking union-nationalists in the 1950s were to reunite the two territories and pursue the ultimate Cameroonian dream. The New Cameroon was envisaged to:

- Build a genuine bilingual ethos.
- Bridge the gap in the development of the English and French-speaking sectors.
- Work for the evolution of a New Cameroonian people from the different breeds of thoughts and actions of its francophone and Anglophone children.
- And create a democratic, liberal, free, progressive, united, strong and developed Kamerunian nation.

Leading exponents of this Cameroonian dream were Ruben Um Nyobe, Felix Moumie, Albert Kingue, Ernest Ouandie, Leonard Bouli, Etienne Libai, Osende Afana, Nde

Ntumazah and John Ngu Foncha. The majority of Cameroonians looked up to those legends of their times in the struggle to realize the Cameroonian dream propounded by Martin Paul Samba.

Imagine what Cameroon would have been today had its liberation fighters and union-nationalists been allowed to their devices to build the post-independence Cameroon. That was never the case. France was determined never to let go of its control of Cameroon, its African pearl. The French imposition of the system that persists in Cameroon today, and the installation of the puppet Ahidjo regime concretized the French plot that preceded the banning of the UPC in 1955.

This ruthless ten-year war to eliminate all aspects of UPC influence in the country, a genocidal campaign that saw the deaths of close to a million Cameroonians in the hands of French and Ahidjo forces resulted in an effective defeat of Cameroon's union-nationalists in the second phase of the Cameroonian struggle for independence, democracy, enlightenment, progress, and development. Ruben Um Nyobe, Felix-Roland Moumie, Osende Afana, Ernest Ouandie and several others in the UPC leadership were eliminated and the rest were either hounded into exile or cowed into capitulation by the French military and the puppet regime they put in place in Cameroon under Ahmadou Ahidjo. It was the death, exile, and capitulation of the heads of the second phase of the Cameroon Struggle and the smug complacency of the Cameroonian people that began Cameroon's infantile malady, a malady that has replaced hopes from a dream with fear and despair instead.

Imagine what Cameroon would have become had Anglophone and francophone union-nationalists realized its reunification, independence, and governance. Had that been the case, the following would have happened:

- The New Cameroon would have been born with an authentic and firm foundation.
- Cameroonians would have realized most of the union dreams (the objectives of reunification and independence).
- And in no way would the pressing legacies of partition still be as glaring as they are today.
- The continuation of the UPC liberation war against the persistent French army in Cameroon and the post-independence Cameroonian army of Francophiles(pseudo-nationalists) would have been avoided.
- Then the deaths of close to a million Cameroonians in the hands of Ahidjo and French troops would not have happened, a nightmarish genocide that still haunts Cameroonians. Those deaths imbued Cameroonians with a sense of skepticism, cynicism, despondency, treachery, dishonesty, and self-centeredness; and traumatized them into a state of political lethargy.

Today, most Cameroonians agree that the human obstacles to nation building lie more in the fact that reunification and independence were achieved by good-intentioned Anglophone union-nationalists and a

Francophile Ahidjo regime that had little respect and knowledge of Anglophone aspirations and the collective Cameroonian dream (the objectives of reunification and independence). Ahidjo was put in power to defend the interest of those in the French political establishment, his collaborators, and his ego. He was prepared to do that at all cost. Yes, it is this legacy of power retention, oppression, and division that the Biya regime inherited and is excessively, shamelessly and madly strengthening in order to maintain his hold onto power. Yes, the shameful Ahidjo regime betrayed the dream of reunification and independence and conceived of the virus of distrust, disintegration, and dishonesty that the Biya regime has proliferated to suffocate the cherished Cameroonian nation-state. This is a virus that has almost eroded our dynamic spirit and progressive values, leaving us with the looming specter of despondency, which threatens to doom Cameroon.

The reunification spirit and its all-embracing dream were the dominant factors in our political lives before the quasi-independence/reunification of the land. Nevertheless, it was the Anglophone community led by English-speaking union-nationalists who realized reunification. The role of Anglophone union-nationalists is the most patriotic to have been realized and the entire force of Cameroon's Union-Nationalism holds the people of the former British Southern Cameroons highly for that. Still, the ultimate Cameroonian dream, which is the responsibility of both English-speaking and French-speaking Cameroonians, has not been realized. The responsibility for that setback lies entirely with the French political establishment, Francophile regimes of Ahidjo and Biya, and their Anglophone collaborators. The unfortunate thing is that the Anglophone community has been the most betrayed. However, we must be honest with ourselves by accepting the fact that the entire Cameroonian people have been betrayed by the French-imposed system and that in our different ways, we too contributed to the success of the French-imposed regimes.

Today, it is getting to five years since the resurgence of Cameroon's union-nationalism. However, the years of lethargy still haunt the Cameroonian people. The questions now are:

- Must we allow the Cameroonian dream to die?
- Must we allow the realistic beliefs of the majority of Cameroonians for almost a century to end up as an illusion because France and its accomplices of unpatriotic and anti-nationalists Cameroonians do not cherish them?
- Must we allow Cameroon to disintegrate and fail the drive for reunification that was given a positive response in the 1961 plebiscite by British Southern Cameroonians, and gallantly fought for by the majority of former French-Camerounians, just because a treacherous minority that constitutes the French-imposed establishment does not care?

- • Must we allow despair to overwhelm our century-old dream and us?
- • Should we betray our fallen legends and heroes because the price for rejecting the French-imposed system is too high?

No, the union-nationalists of Cameroon would not. They would not betray their ancestors, their dream, their heroes, their history of resistance and themselves.

Cameroonians would not surrender to despondency. They would continue the struggle against the oppressive and exploitative political influences in Cameroon in the guise of the current system. They would continue relentlessly in the struggle to eliminate the destructive aspects of the years of partition and Ahidjo-Biya rules.

Cameroonians would never surrender in the struggle against the anachronistic French-imposed system and the Biya regime. They are determined to continue in the struggle to eradicate the disheartening despair, division, cynicism, dishonesty and self-centeredness that have gripped the once noble Cameroonian soul. That is the will of the union-nationalists.

They are determined to continue hoisting the flag of the Cameroonian struggle to a logical conclusion. That commitment is not a matter of words. It is a difficult, demanding and selfless struggle—a task demanding actions, sacrifices and steadfastness. If we all get out of our lethargy and join the cause, all would soon be won; and we would not regret that we failed to save our nation from disintegration. That can be achieved only after we have discarded our self-centered attitudes and banish the negative legacies of partition and Ahidjo-Biya rules to the dustbin of history.

November 4, 1994   Janvier Tchouteu

Chapter Three

The Geopolitical Evolution of Germany and Cameroon compared

Cameroon (Kamerun) being a defeated territory during World War One suffered the same fate as its defeated former colonial master (Germany) and their paths to unification and reunification are identical, which makes them analogous. So I hope this analogy makes things less hazy for readers.

Otto von Bismarck pushed for German unification through "blood and iron" (culminating in the Franco-Prussian War of July 19, 1870 – May 10, 1871) and skillful understanding of *realpolitik*, so that the princes of the various German states led by Prussia, proclaimed the German nation-state *Deutschland* with Wilhelm I of Prussia as German Emperor. This was done on 18 January 1871, in the Hall of Mirrors at the Palace of Versailles, France, following the capitulation of France. France lost Alsace and Lorraine (French provinces with ethnic German majorities) to Germany from that defeat. A decade later, the unified German nation-state brought together (united) villages, tribes, ethnic groups, traditional African kingdoms (*chefferies or fondoms, sultanates and lamidates* into the German protectorate and later colony popularly called

Kamerun. In 1911, following the Agadir crisis in Morocco where Germany and France were on the brink of war over the control of this Berber territory, France caved in and offered Germany territories that today are in the Central African Republic, Gabon, and the Congo Republic in exchange for Germany relinquishing claims to Morocco. In addition to that exchange, Germany gave a piece of Kamerun to France, a territory currently in Chad (Ndjamena and the environs). This new acquisition constituted what was known at the time as *Neue Kamerun* (New Kamerun). The other big powers did not recognize France's loss, which is why in 1916, following the defeat of Germany in Kamerun, France reintegrated the territories it lost in 1911 into its Central African Empire without a fuss, while administering the part of the former German Kamerun it captured as a conquered territory until Kamerun's partition between Britain and France into British Cameroons and French Cameroon and the recognition of these two territories as Mandate territories by the newly formed League of Nations, which was an intergovernmental organization that was founded on January 10, 1920 as a result of the Paris Peace Conference that ended the First World War.

World War One came to pass with Germany and its colonies defeated, and Germany stripped of its colonies and parts of Germany with substantial non-ethnic Germans (Alsace and Loraine to France, Duchy of Schleswig to Denmark and parts of Prussia and Pomerania to Poland), Eupen-Malmedy to Belgium. In the case of Kamerun, the victorious powers stripped it of the territories Germany acquired for Kamerun in 1911. Then they went on and partitioned the Kamerun mainland into British Cameroons (British Northern Cameroons and British Southern Cameroons) and French Cameroun.

Germany suffered Kamerun's fate of partition after the Second World War when it was divided into four zones of control (British Zone, French Zone, American Zone and Soviet (Russian) zone). Later, the American, French and British Zones merged and formed the Federal Republic of Germany (West Germany). The Russian zone evolved into the German Democratic Republic (East Germany). In 1989, East Germany reunited with West Germany (German Reunification).

In 1961, British Southern Cameroons gained independence by reuniting (Reunification or rejoining) with the former French Cameroun, which had been granted independence (quasi) by France on January 01, 1960 through the French puppet Ahmadou Ahidjo in disregard of the majority wish of Cameroonians on both sides of the Mungo who were supporting the anti-French and anti-British colonialists and who were for reunification before independence.

The deception by Britain and France using the Western tool or puppet Ahidjo, who handed over power in 1982 to another tool of imperialism (Paul Biya) is what is haunting Cameroon and Cameroonians today.

Germany is under the USA's political thumb today, just like Kamerun is under France's socio-economic and political thumb. That is why the struggle for the New Cameroon needs to be two-pronged—France (not the common French people and the Cameroonian establishment made up of Anglophone Cameroonians and Francophone Cameroonians).

February 06, 2018   Janvier Tchouteu

Chapter Four

Africa's Haunted Heart

A specter looms in the lives of every Cameroonian child, man or woman. It is the living president of the land in the middle of Africa, the land that is often referred to as the microcosm of the continent. The specter is President Paul Biya of Cameroon. When rumors spread like wildfire in June 2004 that he had just died, there were widespread scenes of jubilation all across the half a million square kilometer landmass called Cameroon. Days after the circulation of the unverified account, he returned home from abroad where he had been passing his time, intermittently, about six months every year for over two decades, and then declared to the sycophants waiting to receive him at the airport that there would be a .... "Rendez-vous in 20 years' time with those who wish me dead..."

Cameroonians were not the only ones who disbelieved him when he made that pronouncement among other things. Many of those who follow political developments in the world in general, and in Africa and Cameroon in particular, marveled at his audacity. After all, more than 80% of the Cameroonian population loathed his rule; he was already in power for more than two decades as the head of state, after having been the country's prime minister (1972-1982) or the second most powerful person in the system put in place in Cameroon by the French overlords.

But Paul Biya proved everyone wrong. He pulled off another electoral charade and declared himself the winner in the October 2004 presidential election, and then changed his constitution in 2008 that would allow him to run for two more presidential 7-year terms (despite the deaths of 150 protesting Cameroonians caused by his armed forces), meaning that he could be president until the year 2025 (a record of 43 years in power) when he would be 92 years of age.

That explains why by the time Paul Biya held another masquerade called presidential elections in October 2011, he had already successfully humbled the internationally recognized opposition heads (who are all former members of the country's sole political party from 1972-1990, a party Biya has been leading since 1984), promised to give them positions in his government and made it known in plain terms that the system string-controlled by the puppeteer (France) would never allow political change in Cameroon that would curtail France's unrestricted interests in the African country.

The octogenarian Paul Biya is variously described as the Maradona (he fakes and wins elections just like Maradona faked and scored a goal in his "Hand of God" goal) of Cameroonian and African politics, the master of presidential patricide (he devoured his predecessor who passed over power to him, leading to the first Cameroonian president Ahmadou Ahidjo's exile, death and burial abroad—Senegal), the absentee president, the vindictive president, the evil president, etc. etc.

As a German colony from 1884-1916, Kamerun was often referred to by the German Colonial administration and the imperial-minded in the Kaiser's Germany as an "African Pearl", owing to the colony's robust economy, highest literacy rate in the continent in the early 1900s, magnificent physical features, rich and varied vegetation cover, and also owing to its diverse ethnic ethnicities that included all the major language groups in Africa (Afro-Asia, Niger-Congo-A, Niger-Congo-B or Bantu, and Nilo-Saharan. in fact, historians consider the German colony of Kamerun as a major part of Adolf Hitler's rule over the territories Germany lost after the First World because of the peace terms imposed on it by the victories Allied Powers during the Versailles Conference. As it happens, one of the peace terms imposed on the post-Kaiser Germany was the loss of German Kamerun to Britain and France. That was how Kamerun was partitioned into British Cameroons and French Cameroon.

As a matter of fact, the French Cameroun mandate became France's most valuable asset in Sub-Saharan Africa. Its value was validated even further when the territory became the Launchpad of French General Charles De Gaulle-led Free French Forces that wrestled French Equatorial Africa from the Nazi puppet regime of Vichy France during the Second World War. This force would gallantly fight alongside Allied Forces against Italian and German forces in Libya, Tunisia and the Middle East, before carrying on to Italy and France where their biggest achievement was the liberation of Paris. The fact that French Camerounians played an invaluable role in the war effort to liberate France from Nazi Germany makes the explanation simple as to why French Camerounian soldiers returned home and sought self-government, liberty, democracy, reunification with British Cameroons that would culminate in the independence of the two United Nations Trust Territories. They were merely seeking the rights that they had helped France to regain from Nazi Germany, which is why pundits were not surprised at all.

The formation of the UPC (Union of the Populations of the Camerouns) in French Cameroun in 1946 and the birth of sister union-nationalist (civic-nationalist) parties in British Cameroons highlighted the seriousness of the former Kamerunians to work together to build a "New Cameroon". By 1955, the UPC commanded more than 80% of popular support in French Cameroun.

So pundits considered it foolhardy when the French government issued a decree banning the UPC on July 13, 1955, in French Cameroons, a strategic act that was followed by the party's ban in British Cameroons three years later on the same fabricated charges of inciting violence and for being communists. These coordinated moves by Africa's two foremost colonial masters at the time were supposed to spell disaster for the dream held by Cameroon's leaders. Many Cameroonians saw nothing but duplicity and hypocrisy in the moves, wondering whether the freedom they had assisted the Free French Forces to achieve for France and its citizens was a special right or privilege meant for "White People" only.

When in 1956, the UPC resorted to a partisan war of liberation from French rule, it was a belated move to confront France after failing to resolve the ban in a peaceful manner. That war would end with the defeat of the UPC in 1970, a defeat that came with the assassinations and execution of the party's successive heads in 1958, 1960 and 1971, i.e., the deaths of Ruben Um Nyobe, Dr. Felix Moumie, and Ernest Ouandie respectively. It would leave Cameroon entrapped through a French-imposed system rooted in the Colonial Pact France made its puppets sign before allowing their countries to become members of the United Nations Organization by granting these former colonies string-controlled independence.

Despite the period of instability during the country's unsuccessful war of liberation that saw the French Trusteeship masters handing power to those who never asked for or never fought for it (the puppets that constitute the system today), despite the eventual peaceful reunification of British Southern Cameroons with the former French Cameroun, despite Cameroon's agricultural recovery and the discovery of oil in the 1970s that saw the country emerge as Africa's eighth largest economy and the world's second fastest growing in the early 1980s, Cameroon is today in a horrible shape.

The Cameroonian economy that was expected to grow twenty times over the next thirty years, i.e., from 1982-2012, barely doubled over that period of time. Everything changed for the worse after Paul Biya was handed power in November 1982 by the first French-installed puppet

Cameroonian president Ahmadou Ahidjo. Since then, Cameroon has experienced the biggest proportionate embezzlement of state funds ever recorded in Africa. And the country holds the sad record as the country in Africa that has experienced the worst peacetime impoverishment since 1960.

Today, president Paul Biya is presiding over a nation where more than 80% of its physicians are abroad, where more than 90% of its doctorate degree holders are abroad, where Cameroonians invest abroad more than at home, where Cameroonians are voting against the system with their feet; today, Cameroon's neighbors who before envied its high standards of living and saw it as a place of refuge and opportunities, now find Cameroonians envying them as they forge ahead with a sense of direction while Cameroon lags behind in its spiral towards total, complete and horrifying economic, social and political decay.

People unfamiliar with the Cameroonian situation would be wondering why such an abysmal situation persists. Well; the answer is simple. Cameroon finds itself today in a situation like someone in a quicksand because of the anachronistic system put in place by Gaullist France when General Charles De Gaulle returned to power in 1958 and decided to make France's former colonies and territories members of the United Nations Organization (UNO), while controlling them with transparent or invisible strings this time. French Cameroun and British Southern Cameroons achieved independence and reunification all right, only for the people to find that the new country is quasi-independent under a broader French template of control variously described as FrancAfrique. This French-imposed system has traumatized, demoralized, divided and dehumanized the Cameroonian people over the years.

The Gaullist system put in place by the elites of the French political establishment has as one of its major objectives the exclusion from Cameroon's political power of the union-nationalists advocating for the reunification and independence of the divided territories of the former German Kamerun, civic nationalists who commanded the support of more than 80% of the populations of both territories of British Cameroons and French Cameroun in the 1950s and 1960s. The current system in Cameroon is a partnership of French imperial interest in Africa (economic and political) otherwise known as FrancAfrique and its Cameroonian collaborators (the renegades and anti-union-nationalists who never opposed and who do not object to France's neo-colonial stranglehold of Cameroon).

The system has been effective in infecting the minds of many Cameroonians, reducing them into a state of hopelessness, in a process that lures them to direct their energy not against the Biya regime and the system, but at their neighbors. The system has successfully elevated corruption and the divide-and-rule strategy into an art—it has promoted the notion of settlers and indigenes, it has encouraged ethnocentrism, tribalism, clannishness, regional jingoism, sectarianism and other forms of division. We see a total and complete absence of strategic or even tactical planning when it comes to the economic and social development of the nation. We see a complete absence of social solidarity.

To compound the division and confusion among the people who reject the Biya regime and the French-imposed system, the so-called opposition leaders these freedom-craving Cameroonians had been looking up to have now been absorbed back into the system, leaving the struggling Cameroonian masses distrustful of politicians in general. Today, the down-trodden Cameroonian people are in a state of political lethargy.

When Paul Biya called for the holding of Senate elections in April 2013, eighteen years after his parliament promulgated a law to create one, most Cameroonians thought it would be another charade, as usual. It made no sense for the so-called opposition parties with a semblance of representation in parliament to glorify the charade with their participation. Most Cameroonians knew the system was sustaining these so-called opposition leaders financially and that some of them were in the government, but Cameroonians were not prepared for the extent to which these politicians would go to insult their intelligence. But deals between the ruling party and the opposition were made all right. The electoral masquerade took place and the people saw the ruling party campaigning for the so-called main opposition party (Social Democratic Front—SDF) in some regions of the country, while the SDF in the words of its chairman or president John Fru Ndi "…one good turn deserves another…", openly backed the ruling party, thereby ensuring its victory in other regions of the country.

How could that have happened? Politically-shocked Cameroonians have been asking themselves ever since the open fornication between the ruling party and the so-called opposition political parties in April 2013.

To prevent chaos and ensure a smooth succession, SDF spokes-persons, and apologists quip.

"Paul Biya has a deal with the SDF to hand over power to one of its members," some anonymous voices within the SDF echo.

If you ask me, my answer is clear. What was supposed to be a Cameroonian revolution that began on May 26, 1990, became a political comedy played by former members of the French-imposed system or political establishment, a political comedy that has gone full circle. The worldwide wind of change generated by Mikhail Gorbachev's Glasnost and Perestroika that swept away authoritarian systems in Eastern Europe and Africa, and that stirred the vast majority of Cameroonians in the 1990s to risk their lives in the streets demanding political change, was effectively controlled by the system. The desire for change that more than 80% of Cameroonians have has been hijacked by the authoritarian system in Cameroon and the so-called leaders of the opposition. The people got taken for a ride.

The biggest mistake made by Cameroonians was that when the clamor for change began, they followed Cameroonians who had no democratic credentials, people who hardly a year before were in the upper echelons of power in the system, but who at the time claimed they had left the ruling party and now opposed it. All the so-called heads of what the world knows today as the prominent opposition parties in Cameroon (John Fru Ndi of the SDF, Bello Bouba Maigari of the UNDP, Ndam Njoya of the

CDU etc.) were members of the ruling party right up to the year 1990, when the system was forced to accept multi-party politics in Cameroon. Like the Pied Piper, these so-called opposition leaders lured freedom-starved Cameroonians into greater despondence and political lethargy. Such a feat was achieved only because Cameroonian liberals, union-nationalists, revolutionaries, democrats and patriots who had always rejected the system, thought these so-called heads of the so-called new opposition, these people who were the first to make the moves to create political parties, shared the vision of the "New Cameroon" that Cameroonians fought, died and voted for, a vision that achieved the land's reunification and independence (though it has never been real because it got usurped by the evil system that today is under the leadership of Paul Biya and his French puppeteers.), but that is yet to realize democracy, freedom, liberalism, progress, justice, equality and development.

False are the statements by members of the compromised opposition that had they not openly embraced the Biya regime and the system, chaos would have ensued in Cameroon incase Biya exited the political scene. There is no truth in the statement because the system in Cameroon is authoritarian, not autocratic.

Authoritarian regimes are usually coated with a sublime idea that could be political (Stalinism/Marxism/Communism, Fascism etc.), that could be religious (Iranian and Taliban theocracy etc.) or that could be an interest arrangement (FrancAfrique). in Cameroon, the system is built around preventing those who believe in the Cameroonian struggle (the union-nationalists, otherwise called the Kamerunists) from attaining power.

The system in Cameroon is a collection of individual interest groups, bringing together the propagators of French neo-colonialism and their Cameroonian collaborators. Paul Biya is the head of the collaborationists. And in many ways, he has been acting over the years as an absentee president. Meanwhile, the state has been functioning zombie-like during his quasi-presence. As a matter of fact, even though the mortifying arrangement suited the interest of the puppeteers and the beneficiaries of the system, it exposed the system to popular uprisings since that means the beneficiaries of the system are not clearly or functionally organized. With the advent of social media, globalization, the maturity of post-independence generations that never benefited from the system; and with the soldiers of the 1990s phase of the struggle dissociating themselves from the so-called opposition leaders, the authoritarian system now finds itself even more vulnerable.

The authoritarian system would be faced by a new political force that never associated itself with the system, a new political force that embodies the spirit of the century-old struggle for the "NEW KAMERUN" or "NEW CAMEROON" that confronted German colonial control, stood up to French duplicity in the land in a war that decimated more than half a million of its supporters; the authoritarian system would be faced by a new force that embraces the legacy of those who fought, died and voted for the independence and reunification of Cameroon, a new force that rejects all the values of the system that the

French political mafia over Africa put in place in their game plan to control the destiny of Cameroon, a six-decade-old evil system that can only lead the country into abyss.

Now, as the open and hidden collaborators of the system openly embrace one another (the ruling party and the so-called heads of the so-called opposition parties) starting with the recent senatorial charade where the so-called principal opposition—the Social Democratic Front (SDF) and the party of Paul Biya—Cameroon People's Democratic Movement (CPDM) supported each other's aspirations in agreed-upon provinces with guaranteed votes from party members, the system is encouraging the creation of elite groups of beneficiaries who see or think that their political and economic survival rests only in a continuation or sustenance of the system. We are observing the evolvement of a system that is shedding any pretense of limited political pluralism; we are observing the entrenchment of a system that openly views the people as its number one enemy. Such a system then becomes autocratic.

In a nutshell, Cameroon's so-called opposition political parties that are in symbiosis with the authoritarian system are aiding the system in its gradual transition into an autocratic system, thereby ensuring its survival in a morphed form. The rapidly changing system needs a strong man to be truly autocratic. This would be someone who has hands on the job to act as the president, someone who the French puppeteers would like to portray as the benevolent despot.

As Egyptian writer, Alaa Al Aswany said, "The concept of the benevolent dictator, just like the concepts of the noble thief or the honest whore, is no more than a meaningless fantasy."

It is the place of post-independence Cameroonians to reject whatever farce the system comes up with a change whenever power passes down to the generation after Paul Biya. By absorbing former members of his party who for decades identified with the opposition, Biya is trying to give Cameroonians and the rest of the world the impression that Cameroon's opposition is in sync with his vision for the political evolution of Cameroon. Unfortunately, the system does not intend to let the majority of Cameroonians participate or have a say in Cameroon's political development or evolution.

The New Cameroon will be founded. Not by beneficiaries of the system (past and present) but by those who have always rejected it as an evil system that has been leading Cameroon into the abyss.

But then, in founding the New Cameroon, patriotic, honest, democratic, unbiased and progressive-minded Cameroonians would have to reconcile a country where:

- the system made sure that most of its historic figures who dedicated their lives and even died for the cause for Cameroon's reunification and independence got killed and buried like dogs at home and abroad,
- the bodies of some of these historic figures that got buried abroad are missing,

- a few of the historic figures who thought they could contribute in nation-building got sidelined, cowed and humiliated by the system,
- its first head of state died and is buried abroad,
- and where the people have been insulted for more than five decades by the regimes of Ahmadou Ahidjo and Paul Biya through an imposed minority system that sowed the seeds of division, corruption, mediocrity, fear, and despondence that are haunting Cameroon today.

The ideas and ideals of the New Cameroon hatched by the country's historic civic-nationalists and developed over the years by post-independence union-nationalists is Cameroon's only bargain with the future. It is the only nucleus around which Cameroon can reconcile with its turbulent past; it is the nucleus that all the strata of Cameroonian society can connect to in the process of nation-building; it is the only nucleus around which a free, democratic, liberal, fair and prosperous Cameroon can be built. The New Cameroon would lead the country in taking its merited place in the central African region, Africa as a whole, and the world at large. That would be possible only if we confine the legacies of the Ahidjo/Biya regimes and the suffocating French-imposed system to the dustbin of history.

Janvier Tchouteu   *06/04/2013*

Chapter Five

Flag-Burning by Cameroonians who reject the French-imposed System, the Mafia/Police State in Cameroon

The flag-burners elicit a sigh, or at worst a word of disapproval but no rancor from me. Despite everything, the Cameroonian flag-burners are misdirecting their feelings of frustration, anger or disappointment with a government, a system or political establishment that is bleeding Cameroon, sapping it of its creative and dynamic energy and dragging it into an abyss that I don't even want to imagine.

It is natural that those with an unflinching love for Cameroon would be horrified by the flag-burning, but those with a heart and a head for Cameroon are expected to get over their shock and direct their horror instead at the factors that triggered the flag-burning, which is the French-imposed system, an evil political establishment led by those who inherited power or are the successors of those who inherited power from France in 1960, people who played no role whatsoever—whether as moderates or radicals—in the great, patriotic and nationalist cause, in the century-old Cameroonian struggle to found the "New Cameroon", a heroic endeavor that culminated in the reunification of

British Southern Cameroons and the former French Cameroun, a historic feat realized by the patriotic votes of the people West of the River Mungo and the blood and sweat of die-hard Cameroonian patriots of the East of the River Mungo who died in their hundreds of thousands for the independence and reunification cause.

The flag-burning is unacceptable all right, but whether we like it or not, it is an expression of the feelings of people who reject the police state that France and the usurpers it put in power in Cameroon created in order to impose their rule, a police state that more than 95% of Cameroonians reject, a police state that decimated the leadership of Cameroon's patriotic forces, created a culture of fear and double-talk, triggered a brain-brain, suppressed our creativity and dynamism, sowed the seeds of indifference, and bred a culture of corruption, distrust, division, ignorance and incomprehension.

Today, this police state, this political establishment of the ruling CPDM party and Cameroon's so-called opposition—Fru Ndi's SDF, Bello Bouba's UNDP, Ndam Njoya's CDU etc (two faces of the same coin in a masquerade to sustain the French-imposed system) has been sustaining a kleptocracy, a mafia political establishment that is the worst affront to any patriotic Cameroonian, as it pushes the Cameroonian people into acts that many consider irrational.

Do I distrust the flag-burners less than the establishment, the kleptocrats and the puppets that are not only sucking Cameroon dry but have equally rendered it into the arms of forces that have nothing good in mind for Cameroon?

Yes, I do.

The system can be dismantled before the end of the decade. All Cameroonians need are cooperation between the anti-system forces, an embracement and spread of the national idea, a relentless instillment of discipline within the ranks of the vanguards/advocates of change etc. etc...

We should have been able to identify the Enemies of the Cameroonian people by now. They are not (a) particular tribe(s), ethnic-group(s), religion(s), region(s) etc... They are minorities from our midst (family, friends, ethnic groups, regions, provinces, religions). And unless we reject and mentally prepare ourselves to confront them, we would never free our land (village, town, province, region, country etc.).

Who precisely are these enemies of the Cameroonian people. The 1994/1995 works

"WHO THE ENEMIES OF THE PEOPLE ARE AND HOW THEY ARE FIGHTING AGAINST CHANGE:"
http://viewsnewcameroon.blogspot.com/2010/09/who-enemies-of-people-are-and-how-they.html

and

"HOW COMMITTED ARE CAMEROONIANS IN THE STRUGGLE TO CHANGE THE FRENCH-IMPOSED SYSTEM AND THE BIYA DICTATORSHIP"
http://viewsnewcameroon.blogspot.com/2010/10/how-committed-are-we-in-struggle-to.html provide an insight.

Janvier Tchouteu   *August 16, 2017*

Chapter Six

Cameroon's Number One Minority Problem

No matter how Cameroon's inescapable problem is presented by its advocates, no matter whom these advocates direct their fire at, no matter how honorable or dishonorable some of the advocates for a solution of the inescapable problem are, no matter what the cause (difficult to define because of its diverse goals) promises upon its realization, the truth is that the number one minority problem in Cameroon is the predicament of the peoples west of the River Mungo (Southwestern German Kamerun, British Southern Cameroons, West Cameroon, Northwest and Southwest Regions, or what is today Northwest and Southwest regions). The problem was caused by the ill will or bad faith of the evil French-imposed system (the Ahidjo-Biya regimes of Cameroonians who did not support the reunification and independence cause), exacerbated by the docility and incomprehension of Cameroonians after their defeat by the evil system; but the problem would be solved by Cameroonians on both sides of the River Mungo working together to get rid of our living nightmare (the Biya regime and the evil system).

No linguistic entity (Francophones or Anglophones, or the different ethnic groups) is responsible for the plight of the peoples west of the River Mungo. The evil minority system supported by less than 10% of Cameroonians; a system that is rejected by every single ethnic group, province and religion in Cameroon; a system led today by Paul Biya in collaboration with criminals from every ethnic group, province, linguistic entity and religion; is what is suffocating the peoples west of the River Mungo and the rest of Cameroonians in general.

It is along those parameters that we, Cameroonians, can found the New Cameroon where all the grievances of its diverse peoples can be redressed. We can only realize that by closing ranks as victims of an evil system we never opted for.

Saturday, June 11, 2016   Janvier Tchouteu

Chapter Seven

What is the Anglophone Cameroonian Identity?

After watching a debate featuring the redoubtable Cameroonian journalist Franklin Sone Bayen and Joshua Osih (The Vice President of the Social Democratic Front), with the two facing off a host of French-speaking (Francophone) Cameroonian panelists, I could not help but come out disheartened by a fundamental fact—These Cameroonian patriots, Cameroonian civic-nationalists of Anglophone Cameroonian identify who deplore the system's handling of Cameroon, especially its treatment of the land and populations West of the River Mungo (The Northwest and Southwest regions or what was formerly West Cameroon and before that the British Trust Territory of Southern Cameroons, and what was down the line the Southwestern part of German Kamerun), apparently could not be understood in their brilliant presentation of the Anglophone Cameroonian problem. And what was even more disheartening was the fact that most of their learned counterparts were off the mark so many times and even went off-on-the-tangent on the grievances of Cameroonians West of the River Mungo.

The New Cameroon would be able to resolve

Cameroon's fundamental problems, that's for sure, fundamental problems of which the Anglophone Cameroonian problem is the Number 1. But then, what is the Anglophone Cameroonian identity that the other panelists failed to get?

In a nutshell, what binds Anglophone Cameroonians together is something akin to a national identity, an emotional feeling of being a part of the geopolitical entity that is the Southwest and the Northwest regions of Cameroon (the former British Southern Cameroons and the former West Cameroon), a special feeling that arose from sharing a common history, a common language (pidgin English/English), a unique/similar culture, and a sense of marginalization. This sense of belonging, subjective as it may appear, is nurtured by Anglophone Cameroonians grounded on their ancestral ties to the area, or their native ties (having been born in either the Northwest and Southwest), and/or from growing up there from quite a young age, ignorant or hardly/barely conscious of any other identity. A person born and raised in Bangante, Yaoundé, Douala, Mbouda, Edea, Banyo and other towns of the former East Cameroon (French-speaking region)and who studies in English these places, may not develop that Anglophone Cameroonian consciousness or feeling of belonging. This Anglophone Cameroonian identity does not hinder a person from being a Cameroonian Union-Nationalist (Cameroonian civic-nationalists). in fact, most Anglophone Cameroonians and most Francophone Cameroonians are Union-Nationalists, unlike the pseudo-nationalists that make up the political establishment (The

CPDM elites and the elites of the so-called opposition—SDF, UNDP, CDU etc.) in Cameroon today, the French-imposed system stirred yesterday by the Ahidjo regime and today by the Biya regime; a system that has collaborators from all the religions, ethnic groups or tribes, regions of the country. And in fact, the Anglophone Cameroonians who want a separate state for the land West of the River Mungo are a minority.

Cameroonians should not be alarmed by the protesters in the streets of Buea, Bamenda and other towns and cities of the Northwest and Southwest regions. They are the unsilenced voices of patriotic Cameroonians who reject the French-imposed system, the Biya regime and their perception of Cameroonians as a people that cannot set themselves free from tyranny. Cameroonians from other parts of the country should echo this voice of protest and resuscitate the honorable cause to found the "NEW CAMEROON". Cameroonians should all join hands irrespective of religion, ethnicity, tribe, region and other special interests, and then march forward and dismantle this system once and for all, so that we can all begin the arduous task of building the country that our forefathers fought and died for, and voted for in the struggle for independence and reunification. We have an opportunity to build the Ideal Cameroon that filled the dreams of Martin Paul Samba, Rudolf Manga Bell, Ruben Um Nyobe, Felix-Roland Moumie, Osende Afana, Albert Kingue, Ernest Ouandie, EML Endeley, John Ngu Foncha, Ndeh Ntumazah etc. This would be an inclusive nation that would be the light of Africa, instead of the black sheep that

Cameroon under Paul Biya and the anachronistic French-imposed system, is today.

Wednesday, November 30, 2016   Janvier Tchouteu

Chapter Eight

Addressing "Anglophone Cameroon's" Grievances and the Founding of "The New Cameroon"

The disillusionment, frustration and anger of the peoples West of the River Mungo (former British Southern Cameroonians, former West Cameroonians)—native-born and or indigenous (aboriginal) over the bad treatment they have been receiving in the hands of the usurper system (establishment), a system that is not a reflection of the post-independence government their forefathers had in mind when they voted for independence through (re)unification with the former French Cameroun(that became La Republique du Cameroun—the Republic of Cameroun on January 01, 1960) is real, should not be taken lightly and should be addressed in a serious manner. The Biya regime, like its predecessor the Ahidjo regime, and the French-imposed system as a whole, loses any sense of relevance for their gross mismanagement of the reunification and independence project, that half a million Cameroonian civic-nationalists(union-nationalists) and their supporters died fighting for against French colonialism and neocolonialism and the political establishment France set up in Cameroon for its puppets who never fought for, never campaigned for, and never supported the reunification and independence of the lands of the former German Kamerun (British Cameroons and French Cameroun). So, it is not surprising that the usurper Biya regime, which is the second phase of the oppressive and suppressive system France put in place the country to secure its irrational interests its mafia elites pursue with impunity, is bent on subjugating the last patriotic and civic-nationalists force that made Cameroon's reunification possible (The people of the former Southern Cameroons).

Every opportunity to mitigate or resolve the grievances of Anglophone Cameroonians West of the River Mungo should be seized, even though Cameroonian civic-nationalists (union nationalists who honor our forefathers who fought and died for and who voted for the reunification and independence of the lands of the former German Kamerun), believe that an optimal resolution of the Anglophone problem would be realized under a New Cameroon where the anachronistic French-imposed system has been totally and completely dismantled and where the original objectives of reunification and independence would be the cornerstone of building a Cameroon that is progressive, liberal, free, democratic, just and prosperous.

However, even as we set our sights on this optimal or partial solutions, even as we denounce the French-imposed establishment made up of French-puppets and their collaborators drawn from every region, from every ethnic group, from every religion, and from every linguistic entity in the land; even as we oppose this establishment led and dominated in Cameroon by French-favored groups, we should always bear in mind the fact that the establishment is rejected by the vast majority in all the regions, all the ethnic groups, all the religions and all the linguistic entities in the land. That way, the fight to restore the full rights of the people of the former West Cameroon does not become a fight between Anglophones and Francophones; that way, a rejection of the system does not mean Cameroonians hold the Beti-Fang peoples or the Fulani peoples responsible for the Biya and Ahidjo regimes; that way, the grievances of Cameroonians against France's underhanded control of Cameroon does not become translated into a perception of France as an enemy, but rather as a country with the potential of becoming Cameroon's best friend if it makes amends as a moral nation that got led by governments of bad faith that made it fail to become a genuine partner, a France that only needs to turn things around and reconcile with a people whose open heart can even accommodate France as a "Brotherly Nation".

Such a prospect of founding this "New Cameroon" would require honesty, genuineness, and adherence to historical truths from all the parties. The French puppets in Cameroon would have to stop parlaying the distorted history of Cameroon that the anti-Cameroonian forces in the governments of France dished out for them to serve to the Cameroonian people, anti-people narratives that succeeded in brainwashing so many over the decades, lies that denigrated the noble and honorable sacrifices Cameroonian civic-nationalists made for the land's reunification and independence. And even the Anglophobes and Francophobes, and even the Anglophone nationalists and Francophone nationalists (minorities on both sides of the River Mungo) who do not cherish the original goals of reunification and independence would need to cease trying to make enemies out of Anglophone Cameroonians and Francophone Cameroonians.

It does not help when we make comparisons of Cameroon, whose situation is unique in the world, with other countries. Cameroon still has the potential to become the pride of Africa or the curse of the continent. The New Cameroon would become the model around which the future "New Africa would be built. Cameroon stands to become "The Light of Africa". We should not allow the detractors to take our eyes away from the source of that light—Cameroonian Union-Nationalism, whose extension is African civic-nationalism, the nucleus of the future African economic Union and political confederacy.

Sunday, November 27, 2016   Janvier Tchouteu

Chapter Nine

The Case for an Independent former British Southern Cameroons Compared to Others

As indicated before, Cameroon's case is unique...In the case of Quebec and Eritrea, they were incorporated into British Canada and Ethiopia as "trophies of war", hence they could or can politely get out (through a plebiscite or referendum) —Quebec, or fight their way out—Eritrea. Eritrea did just that. Britain simply brought South Sudan and Sudan together, two entities that had no history before as a single entity; and it had to take decades of war and millions of deaths for the international community to allow a referendum that allowed South Sudan to go its separate way. And of course, Zanzibar was a British protectorate (a protectorate which in modern international law, is a dependent territory that has been granted local autonomy and some independence while still retaining the sovereignty of a greater sovereign state. The United Kingdom never granted independence to Zanzibar because it never had sovereignty over Zanzibar. the UK simply ended the Protectorate and made provision for full self-government in Zanzibar as an independent country within the Commonwealth. It was the revolutionary government that came to power a month after Zanzibar's independence by overthrowing the pro-British monarch that negotiated a union with Tanganyika, forming a new country called Tanzania. So, Zanzibar could have stayed independent if it wanted to. Southern Cameroons never had that option.

The case in Africa you could have even compared to British Southern Cameroons's was British Somaliland. Somalis, who had never been united before found their homeland even more divided into three Somali colonial territories (French Somaliland, Italian Somaliland, and British Somaliland.) during the partition of Africa, and the rest as a part of Kenya (North-east Kenya) and Ethiopia (Ogaden). Italian Somaliland became a British Trust Territory, like British Cameroons (British Northern Cameroons and British Southern Cameroons) after World War 2, which Britain administered separately from its protectorate British Somaliland. The Legislative Council of British Somaliland passed a resolution in April 1960 requesting independence and union with the Trust Territory of Somaliland (the former Italian Somaliland), which was scheduled to gain independence on 1 July that 1960. The leaders of British Somaliland and the former Italian Somaliland met and agreed to form a unitary state. However, Britain ended its control over British Somaliland five days before the scheduled unification date, so that the territory was briefly independent as the State of Somaliland before uniting on July 01, 1960 with the Trust Territory of Somaliland (the former Italian Somaliland) to form the Somali Republic (Somalia).

Curiously enough, the descent of Somalia into chaos that made it a failed state following the exit from power of

President Siad Barre, the civil war and the breakdown of the central government, made it possible for a geopolitical entity to emerge in May 1991, calling itself the "Republic of Somaliland", and regarding itself as the successor to the former British Somaliland as well as to the State of Somaliland (the short-lived independent state of five days). Yet no country or international organization recognizes it until today. And there are tons of other nominally independent states that are still unrecognized today who sacrificed blood to secede from the dominant state they were a part of—Nagorny Karabakh, Transnistria, Donetsk People's Republic, Lugansk People's Republic, and until 2008 Abkhazia and South Ossetia (That Russia and a few countries recognized following the Russo-Georgian war) and Kosovo (recognized by many Western countries), but not by up to half of the world.

In a nutshell, the retarding establishment can only address the grievances of Cameroonians West of the Mungo piecemeal. But a true, fundamental, genuine and overall resolution of Cameroon's No 1, minority problem is possible only in a New Cameroon, a New Cameroon that is possible after all the peoples of Cameroon, irrespective of religion, region, ethnicity or linguistic affiliation join hands and with all seriousness dismantle this French-imposed system that has kept all Cameroonians in a cesspool for close to six decades.

And truth be told, I think the Northwest region is the least conscious of that reality as its politicians confuse the population into continuing the embrace of conflicting forces that divides the ranks of exponents of change there, making them to strike blindly most of the time, so that the formidable energy that the region generates gets scattered instead of being fully galvanized and channeled to effect cooperation with other forces of change in Cameroon and in building the broader energy that can sweep this monstrous system out of power and realize the New Cameroon. We need to be critical and self-critical, we need to listen to the points of view of others, be open-minded, start calling a spade a spade and turn our backs away even from our family members and tribesmen who are helping to sustain the system in a symbiosis that is leading Cameroon into the abyss. "Long Sense" is not the way forward. It is anachronistic in the cause to found the "New Cameroon" because its smacks of deception and dishonesty that a rational mind finds intolerable.

Monday, November 28, 2016   Janvier Tchouteu

Chapter Ten

Hopes of Dismantling the French-imposed System in Cameroon, of Neutralizing the Parasitic Political Establishment and of Ending the Biya Regime

The struggle to dismantle the French-imposed system and the Biya regime is winnable. And this quest for change is a continuation of Cameroon's civic-nationalist struggle that began in the late 1940s, which is broad-based and devoid of illusions. The most any other struggle can achieve is a stalemate (military wise) that in reality would sustain the system even in the absence of Paul Biya, give it some life for a while, even though it would be less effective in governing Cameroon, especially Anglophone Cameroon. Meanwhile, it would be devastation for Anglophone Cameroon.

So any strategy should be geared towards a broad alliance and a link with reality (taking into account Cameroonian and world realities). Unfortunately, world realities are things most Cameroonians, especially the leadership for an independent Anglophone Cameroon, or what was the former West Cameroon, the former British Southern Cameroons and the former German Südwesten Kamerun (to be called Ambazonia) are naive about. I am beginning to see a dawning realization though. German

Kamerun was considered and treated as a conquered territory by the Western powers, and none of them appreciated the Kamerunian civic-nationalist ideal of reunification, much less the audacity to pick up arms against "The Gods". All of the Western powers conditioned by their dread of the Soviet Union (USSR) and communism, thought Cameroonians leaned towards the East. And they are allies who will always stick together.

The question for Cameroonians dehumanized by the six-decade French-imposed system and the dictatorships of their puppets Ahmadou Ahidjo (Prime Minister from 1958-1960 and president or Head of State from 1960-1982) and Paul Biya (1972-1982 as Prime Minister and 1982- today as president or Head of State) is:

1. How can Cameroonians rebuild the broad-based alliance against the system accomplished in the early 1990s, when civic-nationalists who before had identified with the UPC, joined the SDF and made it a national civic-nationalist party that fully embraced the dream of the "NEW CAMEROON", the "New Cameroon" dream that fueled the UPC struggle against France and its puppet Ahidjo, the "New Cameroon" dream that fired the imaginations of KNDP, OK etc into campaigning and voting for reunification, the civic-nationalist path that continued rejecting the Ahidjo and Biya regimes (The French-imposed system) even after UPC, KNDP, SDF etc. renegades conciliated with the

system, making them accomplices as the system continues leading Cameroon into abyss?

2. How can Cameroonians rebuild that broad-based national alliance that is instinctively Cameroonian and that strives to build the New Cameroon which would take into account the Hopes, Dreams, Reservations, Fears, Concerns, strengths of the different peoples of Cameroon, while heeding the threats (internal and external) confronting our heavily traumatized country, is Cameroon's only bargain with the future?

3. And how do the advocates for change then work together to dismantle the system and build the "New Cameroon" that began in 1910 as a cause led by Martin Paul Samba and Rudolf Douala Manga Bell, a cause that is in its fourth phase after three unsuccessful attempts, all thwarted by foreign powers lording it over Cameroon.

And the sooner those who believe they are equipped to lead realize that, then the better for themselves and Cameroonians. That realization would be a psycho-social advancement very few who claim leadership qualities can ascend to.

Janvier Tchouteu   *May 17, 2018*

Chapter Eleven

Advocates of the Future New Cameroon

Anybody who is not aggrieved by the traumas that the Cameroonian people have experienced in their one-hundred-and-twenty-five-year history(German colonization and pacification, Anglo-French partition and pacification, disproportionate contribution of manpower and resources to the Free French Forces in liberating Francophone Africa and France, the decimation of the population for standing up to French duplicity over the cause of reunification and independence—UPC-failed liberation, the betrayal of the people in their reunification dream, the half a century French-imposed anachronistic system, the dictatorships of Ahidjo and Biya, and the subjugation and dehumanization of the Cameroonian people) is heartless; but that person who strives to return the land to any of its past states is brainless.

Despite our traumas, our future rests in a New Cameroon that rehabilitates itself from all the ills of its past and harnesses its enormous potentials to build a great producing nation where the powers emanating from its levers of government would ensure peace, prosperity, liberty, development, justice, freedom and security for all

Cameroonians irrespective of their creed, religion, ethnicity, and social and economic status.

Only when the dignity of the Cameroonian people has been given back to them, only after the nation becomes organized to the point where it guarantees a promising future for its children, then and only then would the advanced Cameroonian nation guided by its all-embracing ideal of Union Nationalism, take its special place in Africa and play its destined role in the realization of Africa's economic union and political integration.

Janvier Tchouteu   *February 2009*

Chapter Twelve

Reconstituting the Forces that We Need to Build the "New Cameroon"

Hmm! I see my former comrades of the SDF (a party I quit in 2002), who could have lynched me not long ago for being steadfast in the long-held view (the civic-nationalist vision that dominated the SDF in the early 1990s fueled by the heirs of the historic UPC) that a "New Cameroon" is the only option for us, edging back to the fold, by asking for a federation/decentralization/confederation, thereby acknowledging that secession or separation is unachievable for the lands of the former West Cameroon (former British Southern Cameroons)— Northwest and Southwest regions of Cameroon.

By the "New Cameroon" I mean a new era where the French-imposed system has been dismantled and a federal system put in place, where democracy, justice, freedom, and economic prosperity reign supreme.

I am glad that today, SDF and former SDF supporters who abandoned the goal of a "New Cameroon", are beginning to walk back to the all-embracing national ideal of the Cameroonian struggle. Welcome back to the National idea of a hundred plus years.

John Fru Ndi abandoned the basic tenets of this ideal that encompasses a federation by conciliating with the system, thereby helping to sustain it, and thereby making the SDF a party of the system like Bello Bouba's UNDP and Adamu Ndam Njoya's UDC before that. Once again, the system is incapable of realizing "The New Cameroon". Fru Ndi's SDF, like Ndam Njoya's CDU or Bellow Bouba's UNDP etc, are the two sides of the same coin— one as the face or the head and the other as the tails.

Nfor Susungi and the others—the pseudo-separatists (those using separatism as a strategy to push the hand of the French-imposed system or the political establishment to grant their goals) and the real separatists (the heirs of those who are or have always been against reunification) in the SDF who used separatism as a weapon, unfortunately, put into disarray the multi-ethnic, multicultural and multi-religious endeavor minus Anglophilism and Francophilism that Cameroonian civic-nationalism encompassed and that the vision of "The New Cameroon" embodied, a vision embraced by the historic UPC of Nyobe/Moumie/Ouandie/Ntumazang/Afana/Kingue etc, and the historic KNDP/OK of Foncha/Ntumazang-Mukong. They weakened the SDF from 1994, so that the forces in the party who believed in using the SDF to get "A share of the National Cake" (The Fru Ndi and co faction that dominates the SDF today) abandoned the quest for systemic change, so that those who continued to embrace the quest for systemic change, became disillusioned.

It is those who never wavered in their embrace of the quest for systemic change— those who never betrayed— that the struggling Cameroonian masses can fully trust to lead the New Phase of the struggle to realize the "New Cameroon". They are the Kamerunists, the union-nationalists of Cameron. They never considered the separatists, especially the pseudo-separatists, as enemies, but more as victims too, albeit victims who lost their focus. Even some of those involved with the parties of the system (those in the system or those benefiting from it but do not believe in it) are considered as lost sheep who only need to repent, be "desystemized" ("defrancafriquanized") and take their positions once again as advocates of the "New Cameroon". The process of this reconciliation will lead to the dismantling of the system and the realization of the "NEW Cameroon" we all crave for.

To those who are back, those who are on their way back, those who are thinking of returning and those who are embracing the ideal of the "NEW CAMEROON" for the first time, I say: Welcome Back, You will be Welcomed Back, Welcome!

Janvier Tchouteu   April 09, 2018

Chapter Thirteen

Redeeming Cameroon from the hands of the
Fascist Regime in Power and from Hooliganism

We failed to prevent the armed conflict seething in
Cameroon today, in Anglophone Cameroon or what was
British Southern Cameroons in colonial times, or West
Cameroon during the early years of Cameroon's history as
an "independent" country. We the Kamerunists, otherwise
called the union-nationalists of Cameroon(heirs of the
historic UPC and KNDP/OK that fought for and realized
Cameroon's independence and reunification through the
1961 plebiscite), failed in our civic-nationalist struggle to
kick the French-imposed system of looters and mercenaries
(kleptomaniac fascists per se) out of power in time to
realize the century-old dream of "THE NEW
CAMEROON", and in time to undercut the heirs of those
who were against reunification from saying that "Look,
reunification was a bad idea."

The truth is that the current government, the Biya
regime and the system or establishment as a whole never
cherished the civic-nationalist goals of reunification and
independence that the overwhelming majority of our
forebears fought and died for. That is why the French-
imposed system pushed Anglophone Cameroon to the
wall, thereby giving the heirs of those who voted against

reunification the upper hand to stand as the champion of the cause for the rights of the peoples of Anglophone Cameroon (the former West Cameroon or the former British Southern Cameroons before that).

Today, these two forces that are suffocating Cameroon—the government/establishment/French-imposed system and the separatists/secessionists) that have always been a minority in Cameroon's traumatic history are fighting each other, giving each other relevance—one , falsely as the force trying to keep Cameroon together, while the other sadly as the force to take Anglophone Cameroon away to a future that in reality is Impossible. Meanwhile, the overwhelming majority of Cameroonians who decry their activities are helpless as they drag Cameroon into abyss, making each other relevant in a fight that the powers that be wish for Cameroon and Cameroonians, a people who defied the stereotypes about Africans as a heavily-divided race incapable of tapping into their mutually compatible strengths and opportunities, so as to come together and become a powerful, united, free, prosperous and defensible force. The powers that be would like to say about the peoples of Cameroon: "Look, they are not any different from other Africans. They too are self-destructive; they too are incapable of advancing humanity…the process of their social-engineering is complete; they are fully ready to serve the purpose we had for them…"

The Biya regime, the French-imposed system that has deprived Cameroonians of a say and a voice in charting their destiny must desist from carrying out another election masquerade until at least 80% of the voting age population in all the provinces are registered, until the process of dialogue and reconciliation is ongoing and until the framework of the "New Cameroon" is in place.

The vision of a "New Cameroon" that would be the nucleus of the future "United Africa" must not be allowed to be killed by those who never cherished it, for the sake of our children, for Africa and for humanity. For the "NEW CAMEROON" to be realized, the Kamerunists (union-nationalists), the country's civic-nationalists or those who cherish Cameroon or the original Cameroonian dream must step forward and start the process that would confine the Ahidjo-Biya legacies and the French-imposed system to the dustbin of history, ensure that Cameroon does not disintegrate. The process would provide the people with a federal, democratic, representative and just system that would not only ensure prosperity and dignity for all its citizens, but that would realize the objectives of reunification as espoused by those who fought, died, campaigned and voted for Cameroon's reunification and independence.

Janvier Tchouteu   *April 01, 2018*

Chapter Fourteen

Some Insight into Founding the "New Cameroon"

In the struggle to complete Cameroon's Unfinished Liberation, in the struggle for the New Cameroon, the heirs of the first phase of the struggle led by Martin Paul Samba/Rudolf Duala Manga Bell; the heirs of the second phase of the struggle led by Ruben Um Nyobe/Felix Moumie/Ernest Ouandie/Osende Afana/Nde Ntumazah/Abel Kingue/John Ngu Foncha etc; and the heirs of the third phase of the struggle for the New Cameroon led by the historic Social Democratic Front (SDF) of 1990-1997 where two leaders (Albert Mukong and Dr. Samuel F Tchwenko) distinguished themselves as those who did not conciliate even after suffering deprivations, Cameroonians should be foresighted enough to understand what the struggle is all about, who the enemies or opponents of change are, who are the allies and potential allies and how to go about making ourselves the New Cameroonians and forging alliances with those who crave "The New Cameroon". That way, we get to understand that all the ethnic groups, religions, regions and linguistic entities in Cameroon want change and are potential allies. That way, we understand that the French-imposed system under the Biya regime may be Beti-dominated all right, but it is not the fault of the Beti people who in their majority loathe it too. That way, we get to understand that the Ahidjo-regime was Fulani-dominated all right, but the Peuls were not responsible for it. That way, we get to understand that the heroic legacy of the historic UPC came about from the patriotic sacrifices made by all Cameroonians (Anglophones and Francophones) and that the exceptional price paid by the Bamilekes and Bassas should be factors to strengthen their unity so that it would be difficult for those who conciliated with the establishment (system) to use the hiccups in the struggle to drive a wedge between these peoples.

The New and Fourth Phase of the Struggle for the "New Cameron" that would complete Cameroon's Unfinished Liberation" should be all-inclusive and based on the basic tenets of the ideal that made reunification inevitable and that forced the colonial powers to precipitate our so-called independence.

Janvier Tchouteu   *February 15, 2018*

Chapter Fifteen

Feeling Triumphant despite the Defeats in the last three Phases of the Struggle for the "New Cameroon"

Yes, Cameroonians, whether as individuals, groups or as a nation, need to be proud of the objectives of the three phases of the struggle to found the "New Cameroon" that brought so much pain. The general Cameroonian awakening requires us to embrace our collective history and cherish those enriching aspects of our past, which though tragic, we nevertheless need to emulate in order to realize the New Cameroon. That is what the Cameroon idea or Cameroon ideal is all about. That is what Cameroonian Union Nationalism revolves around.

When Cameroonians fully acknowledge the historic steps taken by Martin-Paul Samba, Rudolf-Duala Manga-Bell, Ruben Um Nyobe, Felix Moumie, Ernest Ouandie, John Ngu Foncha, Ndeh Ntumazah, Albert Mukong etc. at the time, in sowing the seeds of Kamerunian Nationalism, then we can say that we have exposed the foundation or nucleus of goodness in the future New Cameroon; when Cameroonians(on both sides of the River Mungo) hail Ruben Um Nyobe, Osendé Afana, Felix Moumie, John Ngu Foncha, Albert Kingue, Albert Mukong, Ernest Ouandie etc as the true heroes of its reunification and independence, then we shall be able to boast that we have exposed the emptiness of the evil French-imposed system and the usurper regimes of Ahidjo and Biya. We shall even be able to say with unwavering conviction that hand-in-hand, we have established the framework of the New Cameroon.

When Cameroonians come to accept the inescapable reality that the New Cameroon would be born by the active participation of the majority in all the forces of the land, then we can say that we have realized the unstoppable force of Cameroonian Union-Nationalism, which is what shall get rid of this retrogressive system (irrespective of whether it is Biya or his heir steering it) and institute the New Cameroon that would take its merited place in Africa and the world as an enlightening nation for progressive peoples.

Janvier Tchouteu   *November 26, 2016*

Chapter Sixteen

The Case for the "New Cameroon" and the "New Africa"

Paul Biya of Cameroon is regarded in many patriotic circles as an "SOB" for exploiting and allowing his country to be exploited by foreign interests in such a detached manner, leaving Cameroon today as a beggar nation, but he is France's "Son of a B...." all right, and one accepted by France's political allies and the economic powers that be in Africa. Unlike Qaddafi who was not the "Son of B..." of any of the world powers, and so was expendable—given the resources that Libya had; Biya and the system his masters put in place with the tacit or open support of western powers will be defended by France. The worst that the French can do is ease him out of power as they did to his predecessor Ahmadou Ahidjo, and then put in place another puppet that would sustain the six-decade-old system they put in place in Cameroon.

As Howard W. French wrote in an article published on February 28, 1995, Herman Cohen, a former Assistant Secretary of State for African Affairs stated that "The U.S. policy was very explicit, giving major responsibility for Africa in global terms to the major metropolitan powers...The problem with the French is that they never believed it because they extended the Gaullist vision of the U.S. as an imperialist power in Europe into Africa."

Howard W. French (the author of A Continent for the Taking: The Tragedy and Hope of Africa) wrote in the article that "…For most of the period from the dawn of African independence in the late 1950's to the end of the cold war, the United States gave assurances that it was content to see France govern over the affairs of its former colonies as part of a sort of division of labor between Western allies that was aimed at minimizing Soviet advances in the third world…"

Today, Africa, Anglophone Africa especially, and Francophone Africa increasingly, is becoming an arena that is no longer a privilege given to the former colonial masters by an America that was contented to see Britain and France hold sway in the continent; today there is an increasing scramble for Africa by a resource-hungry China and the USA that does not want to lose out to the new scramble for Africa that the former colonial powers are powerless to prevent.

This development is something that must not be overlooked by the African civic-nationalists who understand that Africa and Africans must secure the continent's interest so that its human and material resources gets exploited in a rational manner that ensures the development of the land and the progress and wellbeing of Africans.

Janvier Tchouteu   *2011*

Chapter Seventeen

How Advocates for the "New Cameroon" Can Avoid Distraction and Set the Agenda for Change in Cameroon

It is a pity that exponents of change and Cameroonian Union-Nationalists (civic-nationalists) who are committed to the founding of the "New Cameroon", the almost 100-year-old Cameroonian dream, spend their time responding to the utterances of detractors from the lower rungs of the anachronistic French-imposed system. It is also a pity that some of our advocates of change even thrive on countering their utterances with utterances of their own that mirror the shallowness of their minds as progressive political beings.

The madness of Paul Biya's CPDM should be countered with advanced ideas and logical arguments that are devoid of tribal, ethnic, regional or linguistic blindness. That is our only bargain for the future "New Cameroon".

To further ridicule our intelligence, we have spoilers (confused and one-sided) who immediately excuse the ridiculous utterances of these pseudo-advocates of change who are cursed by a dogged sense of self-righteousness, and who in their twisted ways go about distorting the Cameroonian reality and history to suit their purposes, purposes that are not for the interest of those they purport to be for—the struggling, cheating and energetic Cameroonian masses.

Simply, I am tired of seeing our people reacting to distractions from the regime in power. It has been going on like this since 1992 when the exponents of change stopped being the pacesetter in the struggle against the system. What is abhoring is the fact that while, before, Cameroonians had to deal with detractors at the top of the government, the exponents of change have been so weakened to the point that they now find themselves responding even to nincompoops of detractors from the lowest ranks of the regime in power, and even from people with no progressive and inclusive thought formulations that profess to be in the opposition.

We can boast of setting the pace of the struggle to build a "New Cameroon" only when the regime in power and the system as a whole starts being the one responding to our ideas and actions. Moreover, that would require an effective organization and undivided ranks devoid of spoilers with self-centered personal, tribal, regional or linguistic agendas.

Janvier Tchouteu   *December 06, 2016*

Chapter Eighteen

Politicians and Revolutionaries in the Struggle for the NEW CAMEROON

Politicians are not those who are meant to change a system and take a country out of an impasse into the future. That is the work of revolutionaries.

Politicians operate in established systems and do the job of politicking to defend, safeguard or promote certain interests, be they individual, group, ethnic, regional, linguistic or national, based on empty phrases or through a clearly defined thought formulation (idea or concept).

Revolutionaries, on the other hand, are those challenging a system, expecting to bring it down and institute a new system that would serve the interest of the trodden majority (the suffering or struggling masses). In the cause to bring down the system, revolutionaries do not expect to benefit or thrive from the struggle. Instead, they are prepared to sacrifice everything for the struggle.

The sad thing is that while the Cameroonian struggle to change the system is a revolutionary struggle, most of the leadership in the so-called opposition parties talk of politics and expected rewards even though they are still engaged in the struggle to change the system. That is why most of them compromised the ideals of the struggle with excuses that "it is impossible to live on clean politics as a genuine opposition in Cameroon." There are and there have been Cameroonians who selflessly gave in their worth to the struggle and felt it was dishonorable to use the struggle to achieve personal benefits. They were and are the union-nationalists and revolutionaries.

During my years of involvement in the struggle, I finally realized that the system (the Ahidjo-Biya regimes backed by the French mafia group controlling African affairs) feared and respected these revolutionaries and union-nationalists for their genuineness, unwavering nature and integrity. But strangely enough, the politicians who profess to be in the opposition conceived a hatred for these revolutionaries and union nationalists just because these revolutionaries and union nationalists are genuine and are not like them, and because they look with horror at the deception of the politicians who are trying to live off politicking and in doing so, compromised the struggle and betrayed the aspirations of the struggling masses.

Strangely enough, we failed in this phase of the struggle (1990-2002) because politicians led the struggle to change the system (a revolutionary demand) instead of revolutionaries and union-nationalists who are far less likely to be compromised by the negative values of the anachronistic French-imposed system.

Janvier Tchouteu　　　　　　　　　　*Friday, 15 April 2005*

Chapter Nineteen

Ethnic Homelands (Tribes) in Cameroon that were Divided by the 1919 Partition of German Kamerun into British Cameroons and French Cameroun

The indigenous ethnic groups below straddle the borders of the regions of English-speaking Cameroon and the neighboring regions of French-speaking Cameroon:

- Bafaw-Balong
- Balong-Bafaw
- Bakaka
- Bakossi
- Bali
- Bamileke
- Bamoun
- Bankon
- Banso
- Duala-Mungo
- Mungo-Duala
- Mambila
- Mbo(h)
- Ngemba (in the broader sense)
- Tikar (broader sense)

Conclusion

Nowhere is the hope for the "NEW CAMEROON" glaringly manifested than in the country's National Football Team, which despite the constraints from the French-imposed system (poor infrastructure over the years, poor and corrupt management etc.), the National Football (National Soccer) Team has made Cameroon an exemplary and perhaps the number one nation in Africa and one of the best in the world. The players never corrupted their compatriots but gave in their best despite the odds stacked against them. They show the world that Cameroon has the potential to become Africa's light and not the black sheep that the political mafia France set up in the country called the political establishment has made the country to be perceived as for close to six decades.

Cameroon's Anglophone problem or better put, the plight of the two Anglophone provinces of the Northwest and the Southwest, the area that was formerly British Southern Cameroons, highlights the depravity of the system more than any other problem in the country. Yet, strangely enough, the forces that want to tear Cameroon apart and the forces that are running it down while appearing to oppose each other, help to make each other relevant. But the good thing is that these forces are a minority in every part of the country.

The forces that want to tear Cameroon apart are most visible in the English-speaking (Anglophone) part of the country. This force happens to be mostly those who voted against the reunification of British Southern Cameroons and *La Republique du Cameroun*—The Republic of Cameroun (former French Cameroon) in 1961, and their descendants today. Their agenda to create an independent Southern Cameroons or Ambazonia is not accepted in Anglophone Cameroon (the former British Southern Cameroons, the former West Cameroon or the Northwest and Southwest regions today) by those who voted for reunification, most whom are Cameroonian civic-nationalists, otherwise called union-nationalists or Kamerunists. Most of the Anglophone Kamerunists would like to see a return to the 1961 two state federation of West Cameroon(English-speaking) and East Cameroon (French Speaking) or a federation of ten or more regions or states, just like most of the Francophone Kamerunists.

Unfortunately, the minority Southern Cameroon irredentists on the one hand and the minority usurper Cameroonian establishment set up by the French political mafia (Francaqfrique) on the other hand, are making each other relevant in their agendas as the anti-Cameroonian Biya regime cloaks the patriotic garment that it has stolen from Cameroon's historic union-nationalists and poses as the force that is trying to keep Cameroon together from the Southern Cameroon secessionists, while the Southern Cameroon irredentists undermine the Cameroonian union-nationalists on both sides of the River Wouri by posing as the force that is going to liberate Anglophone Cameroonians from "Francophones and their regime". Only by Cameroonian union-nationalists exposing and squashing the actions and agendas of both the usurper establishment and the Anglophone irredentists would the "New Cameroon" be born.

Glossary

Adamawa	The southernmost province that was carved out of the former Grand North Province. It is a plateau region.
Akonolinga	A town in the Center Region. It is also the capital of the Nyong and Nfomou Division.
Akum	A Ngemba settlement 9 miles from Bamenda along the Bafoussam-Bamenda road. It is also a traditional Ngemba kingdom and the dialect of the people there.
Ambam	A town in the South Region. It is a sub-divisional capital in Ntem Division.
Ashia	Word used by both English and French-speaking Cameroonians to express sympathy, condolence, consolation, encouragement, compassion, harmony, understanding, agreement, thankfulness, and caution.

Bafang
: The capital of Upper Nkam Division and a Bamileké kingdom in the West Region.

Bafaw
: The principal ethnic group in the area that comprises the Kumba municipality. It is part of the larger Bantu group.

Bafedja
: A settlement and Bamileké kingdom in the Nde or Banganté Division, West Region.

Bafoussam
: The capital of the West Region and Mifi Division. Also a traditional Bamileké kingdom.

Bafut
: A settlement and traditional Ngemba kingdom about 18 miles from Bamenda in the Northwest Region.

Bakweri
: The principal ethnic group in the Fako Division, which is located in the Southwest Region. The Bakwerians are Bantu speaking of the Sawabantu subgroup.

Balengou
: Bamileké settlement and kingdom in the Nde Division, West Region.

Bali
: A Chamba settlement and kingdom about 18 miles north of Bamenda, in the Northwest Region.

Bamena
: Bamileké settlement and kingdom in the Nde Division, West Region.

Bambili
: A settlement and Ngemba kingdom about 9 miles north of Bamenda in the Northwest Region.

Bambui
: A Ngemba settlement and kingdom about 6 miles north of Bamenda in the Northwest Region.

Bamenda
: The capital of the Northwest Region and Mezam Division.

Bamendjou
: Bamileké settlement and kingdom in the Mifi Division, West Region.

Bami (Bamileké)
: Diminutive of Bamileké.

Bamileké (Bami)
: The most populous semi-Bantu ethnicity and the principal ethnic group in Cameroon. It is also their mother tongue.

Bamilekéland
: The western half of the West Region, with fringes in the Northwest and

JANVIER TCHOUTEU

Southwest Regions. It comprises five administrative divisions, about ninety traditional kingdoms, and eleven dialectical groupings.

Bamoun   A semi-Bantu ethnicity and one of the principal ethnic groups in Cameroon. Also their mother tongue.

Bamounland   The Eastern half of the Western province.

Bandekop   A Bamileké settlement and kingdom in Mifi Division, West Region.

Banganté   The largest Bamileké kingdom, the capital of Nde Division, its former name. Found in the West Region.

Bangou   A Bamileké settlement and kingdom in the Upper Nkam Division, West Region.

Bangoua   Bamileké settlement and kingdom in Nde Division, West Region.

Bangoulap   Bamileké settlement and kingdom in Nde Division, West Region.

Bantu

A Large group of Negroid peoples of Central, South, and East Africa that inhabits the forests of the Southwest, Littoral, Center, South, and East Regions of Cameroon. Also the largest constituent of the Negroid or Black race.

Bassa

The principal ethnic group in the Littoral Region. It is Bantu speaking. Also found in the Center Region of Cameroon.

Batoufam

Bamileké kingdom in the Mifi Division, West Region.

Bawok (Bahouok, Bahouoc)

Bamileké kingdoms speaking the Medumba dialects, found in the West and Northwest Regions. The principal ones are:

- Bawok-Banganté or Banganté-Bawok is a traditional Bamileké kingdom found in the Banganté subdivision, Nde Division. Much of the kingdom is located in the city of Banganté. Following a series of strives in the early twentieth century, it lost most of its territory to the surrounding Bamileké kingdoms, with its subjects migrating to other areas in Cameroon and even founding new kingdoms.

- Bawok-Bali or Bali-Bawok: An offshoot of the mother kingdom of Bawok-Banganté, founded in 1907 with the help of the friendly Bali-Nyonga kingdom. It is an enclave in the Bali kingdom (*fondom* or kingdom)

Bayangam   Bamileké settlement and kingdom in the Mifi Division, West Region.

Bazou   Bamileké kingdom in Nde Division, West Region.

Beti   Diminutive of Beti-Pahuin. It is also a subdivision of the Beti-Pahuin group of languages and is broken down further into Ewondo, Eton, Bane, Mbida-Mbane and Mvog-Nyenge.

Beti-Pahuin   Diminuted or shortened to Beti, this group of related peoples constitutes the third principal ethnic group in Cameroon. The ethnic homeland of the Beti-Pahuin people is in the Center and South Regions, with fringes and enclaves in the East Region. They are Bantu-speaking and comprise the following:

- Beti (Ewondo, Bane, Mbida-Mbane, Mvog-Nyenge, and Eton),
- Fang (Fang proper, Ntumu, Mvae, and Okak)
- Bulu (Bulu, Fong, Mvele, Zaman, Yebekanga, Yengono, Yembama, Yelinda, Yesum, and Yekebolo.)
- Smaller tribes or ethnic groups Pahuinised by the Beti-Pahuins such as the Baka, Bamvele, Manguissa, Yekaba, Evuzok, Batchanga (Tsinga), Omvang, Yetude peoples.

Beti-Pahuin people are also indigenous in Equatorial Guinea, Gabon and The Republic of Congo.

Betiland   The Beti-Pahuin speaking regions of Cameroon (stretches from the southern half of the Center Region, to the central and eastern parts of the South Region and extend as fringes into the Eastern province), Equatorial Guinea (Rio

　　　　JANVIER TCHOUTEU

Muni), Gabon (the northern half), The Republic of Congo (the Northwest), and São Tomé and Príncipe.

Biafra	The short-lived Ibo-dominated state that seceded from Nigeria during the 1966–1970 Nigerian Civil War.

Bota	A suburb of Limbe, Fako Division, Southwest Region.

British Cameroons	The western third of the former German Kamerun that fell under British control following the partition of the German colony. It comprised British Northern Cameroons and British Southern Cameroons.

Boumnyebel	A Bassa village in Nyong and Kelle Division, Center Region.

British Northern Cameroons	The Northern half of British Cameroons that voted to unite with Nigeria in 1961, following the controversial United Nations plebiscite in the territory.

British Southern Cameroons	The Southern half of British Cameroons. Became part of the Cameroon Federation in 1961 following a plebiscite that resulted in its

	reunification with the former French Cameroun. It comprises the Northwest and Southwest Regions of Cameroon.
Buea	The capital town of the Southwest Region and former capital of German Kamerun.
Bulu	One of the peoples of the Beti-Fang ethnic group with a homeland in the South Region.
Cameroonian Pidgin	Also called Cameroonian Creole or Kamtok, it is the Pidgin English spoken in Cameron. It has five variants.
CENER	(*Center National des Etudes et de Recherché*)—Acronym of Cameroon's secret intelligence service (National Center for Studies and Research)—that was changed in 1984 to *Direction Générale de la Recherché Extérieures* (DGRE)—General Directorate for External Research.
Center Region	Central province of Cameroon. Comprises eight divisions.
CNU (Cameroon National Union)	Party formed in 1966 from the merger of the political parties operating in

Cameroon. It was headed by first Cameroonian president Ahmadou Ahidjo.

CPDM (Cameroon People's Democratic Movement)   The CNU renamed in 1985.

CU (Cameroon Union)   Party formed by Ahmadou Ahidjo.

Douala   Largest city, economic capital and capital of Wouri division and Littoral Region.

Duala   A Bantu-speaking people of the Sawabantu subgroup, they are the principal ethnic group of the Wouri Division and the Douala area.

East Cameroon   The French-speaking federal unit of Cameroon from 1961–72. It was formed from the former French Cameroun.

East Region   The Southeastern half of Cameroon. The East Region has four divisions with Bertoua as its capital.

Eton   One of the peoples of the Beti-Fang ethnic group. Found in the Center

	Region.
Ewondo	One of the peoples of the Beti-Fang group. Found in the Center Region of Cameroon.
Extreme North	A province in the far North of Cameroon. It comprises six divisions.
Free French Forces	These were French and Francophone fighters who continued fighting the axis powers of Germany, Italy, and Japan, even after France surrendered and signed an armistice agreement with Nazi Germany in June 1940. It was formed by General Charles De Gaulle, who was a member of the French cabinet on an official visit to Britain at the time of the surrender. General Charles De Gaulle strongly opposed French capitulation and the armistice signed by the new regime led by Marshall Petain that created the Vichy regime in the South of France, thereby allowing the North of the country to be under German occupation. He urged resistance against German control of France and its collaborationist Vichy puppets. The movement drew recruits mostly from the French empire, especially from French

JANVIER TCHOUTEU

Central Africa, of which French Cameroun was the base at the time, under the new governorship of Jacques Philippe LeClerc. Philippe LeClerc led the Free French Forces' first major victory in the war with the capture in 1941 of Kufra, a town in the then Italian colony of Libya. It incorporated forces of the former Vichy regime in the colonies from 1943 and saw its ranks swollen by Frenchmen after the D-Day landing. The Free French Forces achieved their greatest glory with the liberation of Paris in August 1944, led by the French 2nd Armored Division because it had the least number of blacks in its ranks. By the end of the war, The Free French Movement constituted the fourth largest military force in Europe, fighting against the Axis powers. The right wing political parties in France have been dominated by its members and the ideology of its founder called Gaullism.

Fulfulde (Fula, Pulaar, Pular, Peul)   A Sene-Gambian language spoken by the Fulani people.

Fulani (Fulani, Fula, Fellata or   A mixed Negro-Tuareg people inhabiting the Savannah from Sudan to

Peul)	Sene-Gambia, they comprise three groups namely:
	The Mbororo, Bororo, Burure or Abore who are pastoralists.
	The Fulanin Gida, Ndoowi'en or Magida, who are fully sedentary communities.
	The semi-sedentary Peul people who are agriculturalist and ultimately resume pastoralism, but often form permanent communities.
	Foulanis, Fulanis or Peuls are the second most populous ethnic group in Cameroon. Found mostly in the northern provinces of Adamawa, North and Extreme North. Their language is the lingua franca of this part of Cameroon.
Foumbam	The capital of the Noun Division and the Bamounland. Found in the West Region.
Foumbot	Agricultural settlement in the Noun Division.
French Cameroun	The Eastern two third of the former German Kamerun that fell under the control of the French following the

partition of the German colony by Britain and France. It became a French mandatory territory and later trust territory from 1918–1960.

Garoua   The capital of the North Region and Benue Division.

Graffi   Pidgin German word for a grass field. A name often applied collectively to the semi-Bantu peoples of the Northwest and West Regions of Cameroon.

Graffiland   Cameroonian word for Western High Plateau, Western Highlands, or Bamenda Grassfields. Mountainous grassland region of the Northwest and West Regions of Cameroon. It comprises the Bamilekéland and Bamounland in the south, and the Ngembaland, Chambaland, and Tikarland in the north.

Ibo   One of the four principal ethnic groups of Nigeria. Found in the southeast.

Idenau   A town in Fako Division, Southwest Region.

Kamveu   The local council of notables among the different Bamileké kingdoms.

Koufra (Kufra)	An important but isolated Oasis settlement in the southeastern Libyan desert that was of strategic importance for the North African campaign during the Second World War. Its capture from the Italians by the Free French Forces marked the first major battle won by France in the war, thereby boosting General Charles De Gaulle's prestige and the morale of the demoralized anti-Vichy forces.
Koutaba	A settlement in the Bamounland, Noun Division, West Region. Also a major military and air base in Cameroon,
Kumba	The largest city in the Southwest Region and capital of Meme Division. It is located about 70 miles north of Limbe.
KNDP (Cameroon National Democratic Party)	Nationalist party in British Cameroons. It led the campaign that realized the reunification of British Southern Cameroons with former French Cameroun.
Limbe	Former Victoria. It is the capital of Fako Division in the Southwest Region.

Littoral   Coastal province of Cameroon. It consists of four divisions.

Loum   An agricultural town in the Mungo Division, in the north of the Littoral Region.

Maguida (Magida)   Name erroneously used for the peoples of the Moslem North that originated from the third group of Fulanis—the Fulanin Gida, comprising the fully sedentary Fulani communities.

Mamfe   The capital of Manyu Division in the Southwest Region.

Manjibo   A Bamoun village in the Noun Division.

Mankon   Mankon is a Ngemba kingdom and part of the city of Bamenda.

Maroua   The capital of the Extreme North Region and Diamare Division.

Mayo Tsanaga   A division in the Extreme North Region of Cameroon.

Mayo Tsava   A division in the Extreme North Region of Cameroon.

Mbengwi | The capital of Momo Division in the Northwest Region.

Mboh | A Bantu-speaking people of the Mungo Division in the Littoral Region, with fringes of their homeland in the Southwest and Western provinces.

Mokolo | Capital of Mayo Tsanaga Division.

Molyko | A suburb of Buea in the Southwest Region.

Mora | The capital of Mayo Tsava Division.

Mutengene | A junction town to Limbe, Buea, and Tiko, in Fako Division, Southwest Region.

Nde | Formerly called Banganté Division. It is found in the West Region of Cameroon.

Ngaoundéré | Capital of the Vina Division and Adamawa Region.

Ngemba | The second most populous peoples of the semi-Bantu group. The Ngemba peoples are found in the northern half of the Cameroon Grassland (Western

                JANVIER TCHOUTEU

Highlands), mostly in the Mezam and Momo Divisions of the Northwest Region. The Ngemba people related dialects.

Ngembaland   The Southwestern part of the Northwest Region that is composed of several traditional kingdoms or fondoms speaking closely related dialects.

Nkongsamba   The capital of the Mungo Division of Cameroon. It is also the largest city in the area.

Nkwen   A traditional Ngemba kingdom and part of the city of Bamenda.

North Region   Central of the Grand North Regions. It comprises four divisions.

Northwest Region   A province from the former Federal unit of West Cameroon and the former territory of British Southern Cameroons. Peopled by semi-Bantu groups of Tikar, Ngemba and Chamba speakers. Their compatriots in the Southwest Region collectively call them 'Graffis'.

Nzui-Mantor   Banganté-Bamileké word for the panther or leopard.

OK (One Cameroon)	An offshoot of the UPC after it was also banned in British Cameroons.
Peul	A French term for Fulani borrowed from the Wolof language.
Semi-Bantu	The unique and unrelated peoples in Africa, comprising the Bamileké, Bamoun, Tikar, Ngemba and Chamba peoples.
Sokolo	A suburb in Limbe, Southwest Region.
South Region	Cameroon's southern coastal province. It comprises the three divisions of Ntem, Ocean and Dja and Lobo.
Southwest Region	Southwestern coastal province of Cameroon. It has four divisions. Formerly a part of British Southern Cameroons and the federal unit of West Cameroon.
Tcholliré	The capital of Rey Bouba Division in the North Region.
Tiko	A coastal town in Fako Division in the Southwest Region.

Tonga

Bamileké settlement and kingdom in the Nde Division, West Region.

Tuareg

A Berber-speaking people of the Mazigh group inhabiting the central Sahara from Southern Algeria and Tripolitania in Libya, to the middle Niger and the northern borders of Nigeria. They moved to the interior of the Sahara Desert to escape the Arab invasion of North Africa in the 7th and 8th century.

UPC (Union of the Populations of the Cameroons)

First national and nationalistic party in Cameroon. The historic UPC was formed in 1948. Banned in 1955, it resorted to an armed struggle that continued well into the late 1960s.

Victoria

Former name of Limbe. Was founded in 1857 by missionaries for the settlement of rescued or freed slaves.

West Region

The southern half of the Western Highlands of Cameroon. It is populated by the Bamileké and Bamoun peoples. It is also Cameroon's cultural and agricultural heartland, and is remembered for its historic role as the center of the country's nationalism and liberation struggle against the French

	Army in the land. It comprises the six divisions of Bamboutous, Menoua, Mifi, Nde, Noun, and Upper Nkam.
Wolowose	Cameroonian word for a whore.
Wum	The capital of Menchum Division in the Northwest Region.
Yaoundé	Cameroon's second largest city and national capital. Also the capital of the Center Region and Nfoundi Division.